Long-Reining

With Double Dan Horsemanship

Safe, Controlled Groundwork Techniques to
Build an Effective Partnership on the Ground
and Success in the Saddle

Dan James and Dan Steers

with Kayla Starnes

Foreword by Bo Jena
FEI 4* Judge and Long-Lining Expert

TRAFALGAR SQUARE
North Pomfret, Vermont

This book is dedicated to all the horsemen and horsewomen who have shared their time and knowledge with us, and the patient and forgiving horses that have helped us become who we are. "Thank God for the horse."

First published in 2016 by
Trafalgar Square Books
North Pomfret, Vermont 05053

Library of Congress Cataloging-in-Publication Data
Names: James, Dan, 1982- , author. | Steers, Dan, author.
Title: Long-reining with Double Dan Horsemanship : safe, controlled groundwork
    techniques to build an effective partnership on the ground and success in the
    saddle / Dan James and Dan Steers with Kayla Starnes.
Description: North Pomfret, Vermont : Trafalgar Square Books, 2016. |
    Includes index.
Identifiers: LCCN 2016010655 | ISBN 9781570767401
Subjects: LCSH: Long reining (Horsemanship)
Classification: LCC SF287 .J36 2016 | DDC 636.1/0835--dc23 LC record available at
https://lccn.loc.gov/2016010655

Photographs by Vernon Bewley
Book design by DOQ
Cover design by RM Didier
Typefaces: Merriweather, Proxima Nova

Printed in China

10 9 8 7 6 5 4 3 2 1

Contents

LEVEL ONE

LEVEL TWO

Foreword

Long-lining—what some now refer to as "long-reining," including work both at a distance and close to the horse, as in this book—is for me a very good complement to riding. Why? Because you can work the horse in different frames without the weight of the rider on his back. But it has benefits beyond just lungeing, for example, as you can flex the horse inside or out and make the horse more "gymnastic"—more supple, expressive, and responsive—than you can with lungeing alone.

Long-lining can also benefit the horse as he learns harder transitions and builds confidence and strength on the way toward collection or "super collection." These techniques help the horse become comfortable, in the best way possible, for a future under saddle.

I first met Dan James in late winter 2014 while in Florida teaching a clinic. He came to me looking for input about his long-line work. I was very impressed with what his horse knew about long lines and offered only a few suggestions.

Dan is a wonderfully intuitive horseman. He has a very good feel for the horse as well as an eye for details, which I respect. I have since had opportunity to view his work with liberty horses and have a great appreciation for his talent in that area, as well. Dan has a great ability to be very present with his horses and to stay in the moment when teaching and training.

Developing skill and appreciation for long-lining gives each horseman a new perspective—one that is very important. Contact, feel, half-halts, and balance for the horse can be practiced and perfected with great results possible. Dan James and his partner in Double Dan Horsemanship, Dan Steers, are very well suited to offer advice in achieving success with long-lining techniques in a friendly, easy-to-follow manner.

Bo Jena
FEI 4 Judge and Long-Lining Expert*

▶ *YouTube Tutorials*

Visit the Trafalgar Square Books YouTube Playlists (www.youtube.com/user/TSBbooks/playlists) and look for *Long-Reining with Double Dan Horsemanship* for free, live-action examples of the following long-reining exercises featured in this book:

Lateral Exercises (p. 73)

Warm-Up (p. 82)

Speed Control within the Gait (p. 124)

Controlled Transitions (p. 129)

Lateral Movements on the Fence (p. 136)

Advanced Lateral Movement (p. 144)

Pinwheel (p. 150)

Flying Lead Changes (p. 154)

Introduction

Dan James and Dan Steers are the two "Dans" behind Double Dan Horsemanship. Since 2009, we've teamed up to teach riders how to communicate more effectively with their horses, both in our native Australia and the United States.

Double Dan is a bit different than other clinician programs, outside of the fact that we educate across two continents at once. In addition to training horses for performance and pleasure, we also have spent time in the entertainment industry.

Who We Are

Dan James: My Story

"When I was growing up in Australia, I was very fortunate to start out with Mom and Dad managing a lot of cattle properties, so I was around horses from a very young age. However, the first animal I rode was a milking goat. From what they tell me, I wasn't very keen about riding horses until I was about nine. That was when a pony named Tonto sparked my interest. It's a good thing he did, because horses were the main form of transportation for us kids.

"Eventually, I was able to learn dressage, as well as ride hunter jumpers and hacks. Then, I got a job starting Thoroughbred racehorses in Japan— up to 300 a year. We had 100 horses in work every day. During that time, I was also eventing and breaking-in outside horses.

"Next, I ended up moving to Western Australia, working on a 1.8 million-acre cattle station. There, I was responsible for the horse section of the station, with about 200 horses under my care. In that job, I not only trained young horses, I did shoeing, teeth care, and we had a breeding program."

Dan Steers: My Story

"My background was a little bit different than Dan James's. I was bred in the city. Growing up, the first thing I rode was the bus to school.

"It wasn't until I was 14 that I was introduced to a horse. However, by 15, I was working for a professional trainer, as well as learning about hoof care. I have a certificate of farriery in Australia, and was a farrier for many years over there, in addition to my horsemanship.

"At 17, I traveled for the first time to the United States, to work in the cutting industry. Later that year, I started camp drafting, a sport similar to Western events like cutting, working cowhorse, and team penning, in Australia with my now-wife, Pia. I competed heavily in this sport until I started touring with Double Dan Horsemanship."

1.1 A & B *Dan James (A) and Dan Steers (B) are the two "Dans" behind Double Dan Horsemanship. Since 2009, they have brought their unique brand of horse training and entertainment background to students across Australia and North America.*

Double Dan Horsemanship has been featured in pop culture, like on *Australia's Got Talent*. In fact, we had the first horses on that TV franchise and its YouTube™ clip has been viewed over 6.5 million times, as well as being aired on the show here in America and England. It was a pretty cool deal for us.

We first met in 2007, as fellow competitors at a camp draft—an Australian working cow horse event—in southwest Australia. At that time, both of us had worked as professional horse trainers for several years. The next year, we started working at the same riding resort, which focused on Spanish training methods. In 2009, we left the resort to work with respected movie horse trainer Heath Harris. Heath lives just outside Sydney, about 10 minutes from the beach in an area called Mount White.

Heath has been one of the biggest influences on our program, and it was Heath who came up with the name Double Dan Horsemanship. He also set us on the path to combining our experiences to educate the public.

Dan Steers and his wife still live in Mount White. Dan James brought two horses to the United States in 2012, to expand the program here. Sometimes, we do clinics jointly in both countries, but often we do separate tours on each side of the globe.

Why Long-Reining?

Although relatively new to America, long-reining is a traditional training method in places like Australia to transition young horses from ground work into going under saddle. Like many of our generation, when Dan James was growing up, his father would stress the importance of it. At both of our first training jobs, we were instructed to long-rein the young horses in our care. However, we never really understood why we were long-reining, or that it could be so much more than just teaching a horse rudimentary left or right turns from a bit. Couple that with the sudden influx of American horsemanship methods that happened just as we began our careers, and you can understand how the popularity of long-reining has waned in recent years throughout Australia, and with both of us. That is, it did until we discovered the depth long-reining can go and what it can do to speed along or reinvigorate a horse's training.

Heath Harris was the person who finally educated us about the reasons for long-reining and he discussed exactly why and how he used it while demonstrating it to us hands-on.

First, he mounted us up on green Warmbloods that had just come in for training. If one of those "giants" wasn't well broke and ran away, it could get scary really fast. It became quickly apparent that the more we had these horses bridled up and working well from the ground, the easier it was when we got into the saddle.

Long-reining is a good intermediate step to bridge the gap between leading a horse and riding him. There are a lot of horses that get "lost in translation" when making that leap, so the simpler and smoother you can make the transition, the better. We're not saying that everything a horse can do when being long-reined he will automatically be able to do with you on his back, but we do find it drastically reduces the level of fear and confusion for most horses. And, colts that are taught long-reining progress much faster starting under saddle than horses that are taught everything from their back.

Heath also gave us a lot of off-the-track Thoroughbreds and problem horses to reeducate. These horses taught us that long-reining is equally useful for older horses to build a foundation, work through a problem, or refine the skills they already possess.

Since we started teaching long-reining to the public, we've learned that the magic it works with horses is only half of its benefits; we've also discovered it helps people gain confidence with their horsemanship—no small thing. Long-reining allows you to focus on teaching a lesson without having to worry about riding your horse through his initial response, which could be panic or a bucking fit. Until he has a concept solidly, when you literally and figuratively can step up into the saddle, it's a much smaller transition to ask for the same maneuvers from the ground, first.

Also, long-reining rapidly builds from basic skills to performing high-level exercises. Many classically trained dressage riders at the Olympian level use a lot of long-reining in their programs, as do some elite Western riders.

This brings us to an excellent point: regardless of your level or discipline, long-reining is for you. Everything we discuss throughout this book, and our entire Double Dan training program, is suited for any horse enthusiast. Whether you are into Western or English riding, our concepts will serve you well.

Once you master the long-reining fundamentals we will cover in the following pages, you can choose to advance far beyond our lessons. For example, look at the famous Lipizzaner stallions from the Spanish Riding School in Vienna, Austria. They have taken long-reining to its highest level of difficulty—now entertaining the world, those same maneuvers once saved lives on the battlefield.

Before You Get Started

Now that we've established long-reining can benefit most horses and their people, before you begin, let's discuss the necessary prerequisites.

There are three main components to our training program.

1. The foundation is our *Ground Control* exercises, which are all done with a halter and lead rope. Before you introduce long-reining, your horse should be comfortable dealing with humans in his personal space and exhibit good manners. He should also willingly let you move his feet forward, backward, left, and right as you ask.

   For a step-by-step tutorial of exactly how we prepare a horse for long-reining, check out our *Ground Control DVD* series, available at doubledanhorsemanship.com. In the videos, we show you how to teach your horse softness in the halter, hindquarters and shoulders control, side-passing, backing up, yielding toward you, three-tracking away, working around other horses and livestock, and circling as well as speed control.

   In addition, our *Ground Control* exercises will prepare you as a handler, honing your whip-handling techniques and growing your communication level with your horse.

   This prep work gives you a big head-start in all three levels of long-reining, but especially Level One. You can start long-reining a horse with a more basic education, but you'd better be an experienced trainer who can safely coach such a horse through the longer and rougher learning curves he may well have.

2. Long-reining is our second tier of education. It consists of three advancing levels, which we'll discuss during this book: Level One starting on p. 23; Level Two on p. 81; and Level Three on p. 123 (We also have an accompanying DVD series—*Long-Reining 1, 2, and 3*—which may help you visualize concepts as you read.) Generally, at least a third of every live clinic we hold is devoted to teaching long-reining. We feel that strongly about its benefits. Sometimes, we hold clinics specifically dedicated to long-reining alone.

3. Lastly, we start riding in our *Body Control under Saddle* series. For the purposes of this book, we're assuming your horse is at least green broke to ride. With that in mind, by the time you finish Level Two, you can start transitioning your long-reining training to the saddle. By the time you progress through Level Three, your horse will be doing some pretty advanced maneuvers.

In an ideal world, you would learn long-reining with an experienced horse, in a round pen, with an instructor. However, we realize that perfect scenario often bears little resemblance to what we actually get. This is why we created a step-by-step process to guide you along.

We set up Level One in a way that helps people and horses that have never done long-reining before to work their way through the foundation concepts.

Also, at a lot of our clinics, there is no round pen, which is an ideal setup, but we realize it's not realistic for many. This is why we designed all of our exercises, from the *Ground Control* series on, to be done without one. However, if you have a round pen at your disposal feel free to use it. It can help speed your training sessions along.

Safety

Handling more than 1,000 pounds of moving horseflesh with long, dangling ropes and a whip can be tricky at best, and dangerous at worst. We'll often do clinics with 15 people and horses in an arena, all simultaneously doing long-reining for the first time. If our methods didn't stress safety, it would be mayhem. It would be unsafe to have everyone together in such a tight space using the methods we grew up with, unless everyone arrived as very confi-dent horse trainers.

However, by starting with Level One, you don't have to be an expert. Our program gives both horses and people a chance to build their confidence in a safe environment. Because of this emphasis on safety, we've never had any kind of disaster at one of our clinics.

Throughout the book, we include tips to keep you and your horse safe and his education on track. Most of the first two levels are aimed at building solid handler skills, which just happen to have the beneficial byproduct of teach-ing your horse, too. By the time you step into the latter part of Level Two and Level Three, your actions will be more automatic. This frees you up to really focus on educating your horse.

Let's go through a few general safety suggestions that will apply to every page. For example, prior to attaching a lot of unfamiliar, dragging equipment to your horse, spend time making him comfortable with the sensation of rope touching his legs and moving around him.

Use common sense about where you stand near your horse. If he is capable of kicking, striking, or biting—you are too close! We call this the *Red Zone* (the "danger zone"). If you find yourself within one horse-length distance, back away immediately. In later lessons, as you build trust, communication, and your horse's comfort level, you can get closer. But when you begin, better safe than sorry. We describe the appropriate places and distances to stand in more detail on p. 19.

Also, this particularly applies to long-reining, and especially when you start walk-ing with the horse: We advise getting in the habit of letting any extra rein length drag from your hands, between your legs and straight out behind you. This prevents loops that can trip or tangle you. We discuss this further on p. 37.

Introduction to Tack

Part of confidently and safely implementing the techniques of long-reining is knowing your equipment. So, let's discuss the tack you need when working with your horse.

Bridle and Bit

Starting from the front, your horse's head will be outfitted exactly like a typical bridle, with a bit in his mouth. You should use a snaffle bit. Ideally, it is D-shaped or has cheek pieces that prevent the bit from pulling sideways through the mouth (figs. 1.2 A & B).

 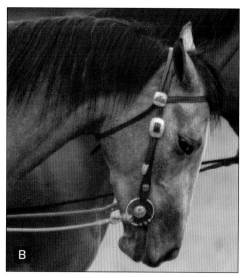

1.2 A & B   *Riders will find a long-reining bridle very similar to what they use for under-saddle work. Outfitted like a typical snaffle headstall, the only major change is the reins, which are reconfigured and lengthened to run through to the roller for the ground-based exercises. Here you see Swampy with two different bridles and long-rein configurations, both of which work for schooling, depending on the level you are working on and current training goals.*

Long-Reins

The only difference between a bridle you ride with and one you use for long-reining is the long-reins, which are about 26 feet long. Long-reins (or *long lines*, as some people call them) are easily found and purchased at most major tack retailers. However, we have developed our own brand of long-reins with comfort, durability, and practicality in mind. They are made from high quality round yachting rope, which slides easily through the bit and roller (see p. 12) to ensure smooth contact and better control. They are outfitted with our specialty Steers Knot for ease of use.

TROUBLESHOOTING

Using the Steers Knot

The Steers Knot is a quick-release attachment developed by Dan Steers for connecting lead ropes to rope halters (shown here) and long reins to bridles and rollers (used throughout this book). Our Double Dan Horsemanship soft leads and long reins come outfitted with this quick and easy connection. How does it work?

1. Begin by slipping the loop at the end of the lead or rein through the chin loop of the halter, or bit or roller ring. The lead/rein loop and knot will sit on either side of the halter loop/bit or roller ring (figs. 1.3 A & B).

2. Then, secure the lead/rein loop by threading the knot through the eye of the loop (fig. 1.3 C).

    This knot lets the rein glide along the snaffle ring, giving your horse a smooth signal and snappy release from pressure (fig. 1.3 D). It also makes for easy attachment/ removal of the long rein when you are connecting directly to the roller (fig. 1.3 E).

1.3 A–E *Securing the Steers Knot (A–C) and two different long-rein set-ups (D & E).*

While many types of reins are attached to the bit with snaps, ties, or buckles, we prefer using the Steers Knot (see sidebar, p. 10). Invented by Dan Steers, this knot lets the rein glide along the snaffle ring, giving your horse a smooth signal and snappy release from pressure. It is always important for the handler to exercise soft, gentle hands when using the reins (more on this on p. 17).

Roller

One of the most important pieces of tack, the roller (or *surcingle*) holds the reins in place and allows you to cue properly (fig. 1.4 A). A strap with small rings attached in pairs along its length, the roller sits on the horse's back just behind the withers and attaches with a cinch (girth) exactly like a saddle. The cinch is tightened about the same degree as you would a saddle's cinch. Unlike the saddle, a roller doesn't need additional cushioning; it is made with padding attached.

1.4 A   *The roller (some people refer to this as a* surcingle*) holds the long reins in place and allows you to cue properly. This leather strap with small rings attached in pairs along its length sits on the horse's back just behind the withers and attaches with a cinch (girth) exactly like a saddle.*

You can use a saddle as your roller in early training stages, running the long-reins through D-rings or stirrups, but this is at a distinct disadvantage to a roller because of the lack of distinct "levels" to place the reins. The best rollers are lined with progressively higher rings, and we believe that the more rings on a roller, the better for your horse's education in the long run. Lower rings keep reins in a relatively straight line from the horse's mouth to the person's hands. Higher rings are for more educated horses, and gradually introduce and refine vertical flexion as the reins are positioned closer to the horse's topline (figs. 1.4 B & C). Long-reining with a saddle just doesn't allow for the flexibility needed to progress to higher placements.

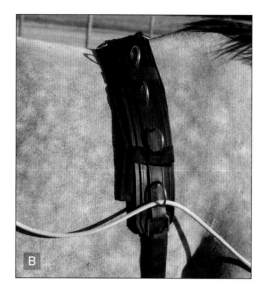 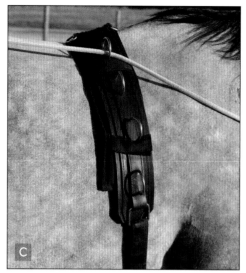

1.4 B & C   *The best rollers are lined with progressively higher rings: lower rings that keep reins in a relatively straight line from the horse's mouth to the person's hands (B), and higher rings for more educated horses (C).*

Lungie Bungie

The Lungie Bungie is an innovative training aid devised by two leading eventing riders—Clayton and Lucinda Fredericks of the United Kingdom—in consultation with leading tack manufacturer Libby's (fig. 1.5). The Lungie Bungie has two strong cords of elastic with a triggered connector and the ability to adjust for different tensions, and the design encourages equal pressure on both sides of the bit, as well as softness. When your horse has reached Level Three in our program, you may want to consider using the Lungie Bungie to help him develop his balance and his frame (see p. 117). Throughout this book, you will see the Lungie Bungie in photos depicting various schooling scenarios as we believe it is a valuable tool when used correctly. (For ordering information, visit doubledanhorsemanship.com.)

1.5   *The Lungie Bungie consists of two, short elastic reins that run from the bit to the roller. It is an invaluable training aid when encouraging collection and the development of a frame. You can use the Lungie Bungie with all different varia-tions of long-rein setups—here you see a more advanced scenario using a ring at the top of the roller. We discuss frame and head carriage in chapter 7 (p. 112), but we'd like to mention here that your goal should not be to "pull" the horse's nose in. Swampy is resting at a halt here and has brought his face a little behind the vertical. When I ask him to move forward I want that nose to come forward a bit as he seeks the constant, soft contact with my hands through the long reins.*

Setups

There are a number of ways you will connect the long-reins to the roller and the bridle as you progress through our training levels, without and perhaps eventually with the Lungie Bungie.

1. In this book, we begin by using a *single long-rein* that's run through the bit ring and attached to the bottom ring on the roller on the near side (fig. 1.6 A).

2. We then progress to two long-reins, both sides attached to the roller and run through the bit ring, back to the hands (fig. 1.6 B).

3. Next the side closest to you is attached as described above, and the oppo-site side run through the roller ring and attached directly to the bit (fig. 1.6 C).

4. Next is two long-reins run through the lowest roller rings and attached directly to the bit (fig. 1.6 D).

5.   And then you may choose to add the Lungie Bungie later in training, in combination with the two long-reins attached to the bit (fig. 1.6 E).

6.   In some places, you may see Dan James using one of the higher rings on the roller (fig. 1.6 F). This setup is reserved for more advanced horses and experienced long-reiners and is not something you will need to use when you initially work through the exercises in this book.

1.6 A–F   *A single long-rein run through the bit ring and attached to the lowest ring on the roller (A); two long-reins, both the inside and outside run through the bit rings and attached to the roller (B—note the scenario shown here uses the upper rings on the roller for a more advanced horse); two long-reins, the inside rein again run through the bit ring and attached to the lowest ring on the roller and the outside rein run through the ring on the roller and attached to the bit (C); two long-reins, both run through the lowest ring on the roller and attached directly to the bit (D); two long-reins, both run through the lowest ring on the roller and attached directly to the bit, with a Lungie Bungie (E); and using one of the higher rings on the roller with an advanced horse (F).*

As you progress through this book, you'll see each of these different setups shown in various places as we use horses of varying levels and abilities to demonstrate the long-reining exercises in our program. We'll explain the best setup for each stage of your long-reining progress with your horse in more detail in the pages ahead.

Whips

Because you are at a distance to your horse when long-reining, you can't physically cue him with direct touch. In this case, you can extend your reach with a whip. We alternate between using two different kinds of whips—a lunge and a carriage whip—which are used for longer and shorter distances, respectively (figs. 1.7 A & B). The exact distance at which you switch from one whip to the other is very individual to the person, but a good rule of thumb is to switch to the lunge whip when you can no longer touch the horse with the carriage whip. It is at this point that he could choose to evade your requests, and you have no way to reinforce what you're asking with the shorter whip. It is important to note that whips are simply another tool of communication and an extension of your body; they are meant to be used humanely, not cause the horse pain.

1.7 A & B   *In long-reining, two whips are standard equipment the handler will have to get used to maneuvering. The lunge whip (A) is for distance work and the carriage whip (B) is used for close-up work.*

Whereas we use the reins to communicate with the front of the horse, we use a whip to communicate with the rear. By placing or tapping a whip on the gaskin area, just above the hock, you can cue the horse's hindquarters to move forward and underneath him. Without much exception, this is the location of most long-reining whip cues.

Holding a whip may feel awkward at first, but it will quickly become second nature. With practice, you automatically learn what works for you. For example, when not actively using the whip, we like to flip the handle around to face it away from the horse. This keeps it handy, tucked out of our way when walking, and it drags along behind until needed (figs. 1.8 A & B). By doing this, you are able to use the whip at any instant, before an unexpected training moment passes. You might miss the chance, if you toss your whip aside to keep it out of the way.

 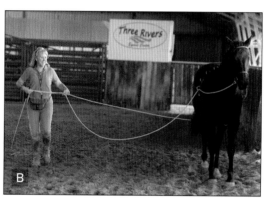

1.8 A & B *While at first you might feel awkward handling the whip and the long-reins, in time it will begin to feel very natural (A). We teach our students to flip the whip so that it faces backward when not in use—it's there if you need it, but out of the way (B).*

Typically, whips are carried in the right hand, but either hand is acceptable. In fact, it is good to be capable of using both hands equally for those unforeseen instances when your dominant hand is not free.

How to Hold the Long-Reins

The most important "equipment" you'll use while long-reining are your hands. With them, you use the reins and whip to make the only direct communication you have with your horse. We've discussed a little about handling the whip— now you need a basic understanding of how to hold your hands (figs. 1.9 A–C). Initially, practice with one rein in each hand: the long-reins should rest easily in your relaxed but closed fingers, both entering between your thumbs and forefingers at the top. As you advance in your rein handling, you can gradually refine your skills to handling reins in one hand for many exercises: either both reins entering between your thumb and forefinger in one hand, or with one rein entering from the top and one entering from the bottom, with your hand rotated so it is knuckles up and bent fingers down.

1.9 A–C *Long-reining, like riding, is a two-way communication between horse and human. Here, Dan James demonstrates holding reins and whip with one rein in each hand (A), with both reins entering between your thumb and forefinger in one hand (B), or with one rein entering from the top and one entering from the bottom, with your hand rotated so it is knuckles up and bent fingers down (C).*

Hands Over Fist Technique

Other than rein- and whip-handling, you have one other skill to master with your hands—our *Hands Over Fist* technique (fig. 1.10). The purpose of Hands Over Fist is simple: it's how you safely lengthen and shorten reins, such as when you alternate the size of the circles your horse travels around you—from large to small or small to large. Without Hands Over Fist, when you reel him in or feed line out, your reins will quickly become a dangerous, tangled mess.

1.10   *Dan uses Hands Over Fist to decrease the size of the circle Swampy is traveling.*

The technique is simple. To begin shortening the reins:

1.   Grip them both in one hand, which forms a fist.

2.   Then, reach your free hand forward and grab the reins just above your fist, and hold.

3.   Alternate your hands up the reins, just like you might pull a bucket of water on a rope up a well. Stop advancing when you are the desired distance from your horse.

To lengthen reins with Hands Over Fist, it's even easier:

Turn your palms up and loosen your grip, allowing the reins to feed slowly through them.

How and Where to Stand

This brings us to a question we get a lot in our clinics. Where to stand? As mentioned in the section covering safety, it is a good general idea to stay a horse-length away when you're not engaged in a specific long-reining exercise that requires you be closer—out of the Red Zone (fig. 1.11).

Drive Line

We should also cover more specific guidelines to help you begin long-reining. To do this, we need to briefly discuss the concept of the *drive line*. Every horse, indeed every prey animal, has an individual drive line. This imaginary

1.11 *Staying out of harm's way when long-lining is all about location. It is important to know the safe zones to avoid a kick or strike. Here, Dan is a horse-length away from Swampy.*

line is that point of balance where if you step in front of it, the horse stops or changes direction, and if you are behind it, he moves forward.

With a horse, the drive line falls from the withers down to just behind the elbows; coincidentally, right where the roller and its cinch are positioned. When positioned *behind* the roller, you will keep the horse driving forward—a key to successful long-reining. Step in front of this line toward the horse's head, and he will slow or change direction away from you (fig. 1.12).

1.12   *Rein cues and body position are the main communication between a horse and human when long-reining. Once refined, even complicated maneuvers are possible, like Dan and Dan driving their horses together without incident.*

Think of it this way: any part of the horse behind the roller acts as a gas pedal when pressured, reinforcing forward motion; anything in front is the brake. The reins are your steering wheel to choose the new direction. Experience will teach you how to quickly step from one position to another in relation to the line to influence how your horse moves. We can categorize your position as it relates to the drive line to help you understand where you want to be, when.

Standing Positions

Let's discuss three positions that you will use with long-reining. They follow the drive-line principle. First is where you stand once you get your horse moving:

For simple *two-reined* tracking, you are pushing your horse forward while you follow along in the more traditional driving stance *directly behind your horse* (fig. 1.13 A).

When your horse is doing *circles* around you, for example in a more traditional lungeing scenario or for canter work, you often stand in the *center position*—that is, to the side of the horse lined up just behind the roller (fig. 1.13 B). Note that this does change as you and your horse advance—you will begin to use the ¾ *position* for circles, and then vary between center and ¾ as necessary.

What's the ¾ position? It is halfway between the first two positions and often used for *lateral movements* and *changes of direction* (figs. 1.13 C & D). Also, if you need to approach your horse—say to give his rump a pat for a job well done, for example, this is the angle you use to do so. From this position off the hip, you can see three of your horse's legs when he's standing still and square; the far front leg will be hidden behind the near hind leg.

1.13 A–D   *There are three basic handler positions in long-reining: directly behind (A), center position by the horse's ribs (B), and between those two at the ¾ position (C). The ¾ position is the position you take if you need to safely reward your horse with a pat on the rump, as Dan James is doing here with his gelding, Swampy (D).*

We will discuss these positions and how they relate to the various long-reining exercises in later chapters. For now, you have the introduction to the reasoning, equipment, and basic concepts of long-reining that will carry you through all three levels in this book.

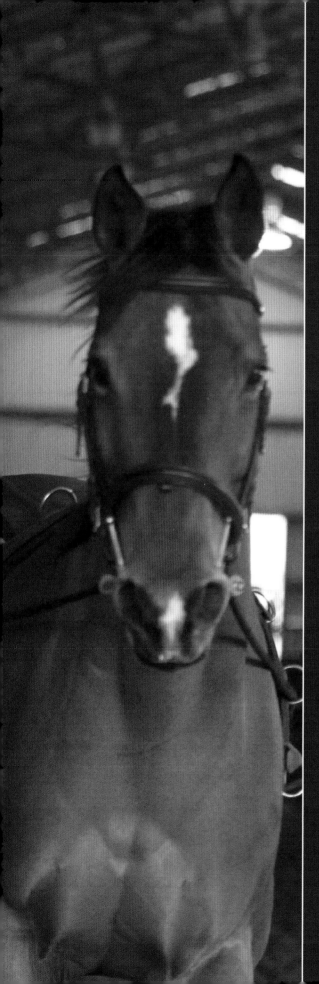

2

Preparing the Trainer and Horse

Welcome to Level One. This is where the foundation is set for both you and your horse. If you have been through our *Ground Control* DVD series (doubledanhorsemanship.com) with your horse before starting long-reining, you will have a significant leg-up teaching your horse to confidently go onto and maintain a circle in both directions, as well as move his feet laterally away both left and right. These lessons will serve you well, especially in Levels Two and Three, where the bulk of the advanced training happens. However, while helpful, learning the *Ground Control* series isn't necessary to start long-reining.

E very horse, regardless of previous training or background, starts fresh here. The only difference in the Level One long-reining program between an inexperienced colt and a calm riding horse is the speed at which you'll progress through the exercises.

- If you are starting with an untrained horse who has never had a bridle on, for example, you will spend more time in the earlier lessons getting him comfortable with the feel of a bit and confidence with the basics. If he has never worn a saddle, cinching the roller may be a desensitizing lesson in itself. However, we do find youngsters that are first introduced to a roller are much more accepting of the more intimidating saddle, when the time comes.

- A veteran riding horse may blaze through these earlier exercises without blinking an eye, but the lessons shouldn't be skipped. They are a great refresher course and may highlight a few holes that can be addressed. They also give him a gradual introduction to the building blocks necessary for what you will ask of him in later training.

Regardless of your horse's training level, you may need to stay in these earlier exercises for a while anyway, for your own education—until using reins and whip to communicate become second nature. In fact, Level One is primarily focused on training the person to become an efficient leader and to use the tools of long-reining, rather than schooling the horse.

Communication and Feel

Before you can long-rein a horse successfully, you must realize it is simply a conversation back and forth between you both (fig. 2.1). You are not just giving commands when you ride or drive. Yes, you are making requests and he is responding to them, but he is also replying with his own thoughts about your cues and his intentions for the future. To explain the importance of this concept to our students, we often have them partner up in clinics for two preliminary exercises: the *Bucket Game* and *Long-Reining the Person*. In both, a horse isn't needed as each person takes a turn in this role.

2.1 *Dan and Dan demonstrate the two-way conversation that develops between horse and trainer through long-reining practice. Both horses are utterly focused, soft, and responsive, but also giving information back to Dan and Dan.*

The Bucket Game

Dan James was first taught the *Bucket Game* by fellow horseman Jonathan Field who is based in Canada (www.jonathanfield.net). Field uses the game to demonstrate to his students how to become aware of *communication* and *feel*. We've already talked about *communication*—that two-way conversation you have with your horse when you work with him. *Feel* is an invisible connection between you and your horse. It allows you to read his subtle, nonverbal communication, from a flick of an ear to a swish of his tail. Feel is innate in both humans and horses. However, where we often have to practice to be able to read horses, horses are born experts at reading us.

The Bucket Game begins with two people holding the ends of a stretched-out long rein while standing on buckets (fig. 2.2). With this small platform as the base of stability, communication and feel become paramount—any tug of the rope from the other person is magnified. The object of the game, of course, is to either collect all the long-rein or get the other person off her bucket.

2.2   *In the Bucket Game, see who can gather the most rein...or get the other off her bucket!*

EXERCISE

1.   Stretch a long-rein between you and a partner.

2.   Flip a bucket over in front of each of you, and step on up.

3.   Each person starts gathering the long-rein until any slack is taken out of it—see who can get the most!

At this point, it does not become a simple tug-of-war where you just try to take rein with brute force. Why? On the ground, you can spread your feet, or lean back to brace into an all-out pull. But, on a bucket, you don't have that luxury and must be more precise with your movements. You have to feel the rein to know when to make contact or when to release a bit of slack before you get yanked off your bucket. Like fishing, you reel in and feed out line trying to anticipate the other person's moves. With feel, you will be able to pull her off her bucket or tug the rein from her hands because you can read her unspoken communication and time your responses to topple her balance.

How does this relate to your horse? Let's take just one possible scenario: a horse that tends to march off too quickly when you ask him to go while leading or driving him. You don't want him to charge forward with too much speed without you having learned feel or it can turn into an uncomfortable situation with you out of balance and possibly out of control.

This is somewhat like one car towing another car: When the car in the lead moves, it can snap the second car forward at the moment the slack goes out of the chain that connects them. This is just like getting jerked off a bucket or getting pulled off your feet when your horse moves off before you are ready. But when you can anticipate a horse's movements, you can react better to them and eventually, modify them.

Remember, the horse is constantly communicating his intentions to you—and horses are always honest about their plans. Soon, you will learn to read a slight shift of weight or the tension your horse puts on the rein as a signal to what he is going to do. The *Bucket Game* gives you a head start with that lesson before you practice with your horse. When you have mastered the *Bucket Game*, you are ready to try the next exercise: *Long-Reining the Person*.

Long–Reining the Person

The *Long-Reining the Person* exercise is similar to the *Bucket Game*—it also builds confidence with long-reining techniques before applying them to your horse. But it goes a step further than the Bucket Game, as it allows you to mimic driving the horse and to learn rein- and whip-handling skills.

Using a person to practice on before you attempt these maneuvers with your horse helps in two specific ways. First, you are not trying to teach the basic concepts of long-reining before you've learned them yourself. A bit of experience and coordination will prevent you confusing your horse and also shorten his learning curve tremendously. Also, by first practicing with a human, you will get valuable feedback about how to improve your communication.

In our clinics, we always have students take a turn both as the trainer and the horse. It gives the driver a chance to become familiar directing with reins and a whip. But, most importantly, the other person starts to have an appreciation of the confusion that can be created by a driver's hands. We've found it to be a very helpful exercise.

EXERCISE

1. You need a partner for this exercise. To begin, your partner holds the ends of two long-reins, one in each hand, and pretends to be the horse (figs. 2.3 A & B). She should face away from you with her eyes closed or be blindfolded so she has to rely on you completely for instruction on where to go and how to move. She should tuck her thumbs into her front pockets or hook them in her belt loops so her reins approximate the same position they'd be when attached to a horse's bit.

2. Stand directly behind your partner exactly as you would in the first position we described for a horse—a horse length away, one rein in each hand and the whip in your right, tucked down and behind you, out of the way (see pp. 16 and 17 in chapter 1 for how to hold the reins and for positioning). The long reins should trail down between your legs and drag behind you.

3. Your job is to guide your partner around using rein pressure and a few verbal cues, such as clucking or kissing. But, before you move anywhere, check your hand position. Your arms should be bent at the elbow, with your forearms and hands forming a straight extension of the reins to your "horse's mouth." Start with your elbows approximately even with your ribs, with only enough drape in the rein to prevent accidental cues to the "horse." You may move your hands forward once you are in motion, but

2.3 A & B *Long-Reining the Person lets you practice your long-rein- and whip-handling skills before you try long-reining your horse. In this exercise, your partner (holding one end of the long-reins) should have her eyes closed or be blindfolded so she is dependent on you for guidance (A). Hold your reins and whip as described in chapter 1. Note that it is important to begin practicing certain safety skills: the tail of your long-reins should trail between your legs and out behind you (B), not to the side (as the student is doing in A).*

the goal is still to keep them close together and make small movements to communicate, much like when riding.

4. While standing still, practice Hands Over Fist (see p. 18). The more automatic you can make reeling in or feeding out the long-reins, the better you'll be able to handle them in later exercises with a real horse, when you will need to react quickly.

5. Practice with the whip. Flip it back out of the way and forward again until the motion feels less awkward. Try holding it in your left hand. Once you are proficient with this, tuck it back and just carry it.

6. When you are ready to actually move forward, return your focus to learning to handle the reins. (You can pick whip-handling back up when you are steady with your rein commands). Ask your partner to move with a verbal cue—whatever you plan to use with your horse is fine. Just make sure whatever you use, it is consistent.

7. Once you have forward motion, try halting, changing pace, or direction. If you find yourself too far away or too close to your partner—and even if you don't—take the opportunity to practice Hand Over Fist in motion.

8. As mentioned, be sure to switch roles with your partner so you can see what it is like to be a horse, receiving cues through the long-reins.

Advancing the Exercise:

Long-Reining the Person with Cones

To advance the exercise, try this exercise, which we will discuss in greater detail and with a horse on p. 66. Here, you can begin to prepare for what you will do with your horse in later training (fig. 2.4).

EXERCISE

1. Set up half-a-dozen or so cones in a line with about a horse-length between each of them. Then, stand with your partner at one end, facing the other.

2. Your objective is to weave your partner through the cones in a serpentine. This will teach you about using your long-reins to signal a change of direction. And, because you are constantly changing direction, you will get plenty of practice. The cones act as a visual aid to guide you along. If you have a clear idea of where you need to go, you telegraph that confidence to your partner through your cues. Imagine a centerline running exactly through the middle of each cone: Your plan is to stick to that path—even though the cones will knock you off course, you have to go around them to get back to that centerline. With a verbal cue, move off toward the cones. As you approach the first one, decide if you will go left or right around it, otherwise your partner will trip. Say you choose to go to the right: Signal your friend with a gentle pull on the right rein. Momentum will automatically propel her forward as well as to the side, which is what you need to get around the obstacle. You may need to quicken your feet to stay in position behind her.

2.4 *Once you can weave your partner through a line of cones without knocking any of them over, you will be well on your way to doing the same Level Two exercise with your horse. Note how in this photo the excess long-rein trails between Dan's feet and out behind him. This method prevents tangling and tripping the handler.*

3. As your partner's left shoulder gets even with the first cone, you'll need to loosen your right rein, slow your feet to stay in position behind her, and signal with a slight pull of your left rein for a change of direction. This will cause her to step left, bringing you both back to your imaginary centerline.

4. However, you won't stop signaling with your left rein once you reach the centerline. Hesitate there, and your partner will crash into the next cone instead of smoothly walking around it, because of how closely they are spaced. So, to navigate the next cone fluidly, simply continue cueing with your left rein to ask your partner to drift across the centerline, forward, and around the next cone.

5. When your partner's right shoulder is even with the cone, cue with your right rein to step toward the centerline into your next curve. By mirroring these arcs around each cone, you will weave through the set.

6. Back when you were both traveling in a straight line, it was easy to maintain your position. However, now that you are asking your partner to go left and right around cones, you will find you need to weave, step by step, right along behind her to stay in position. As she weaves around one cone, you will still be weaving around the preceding one. To do this, speed your feet up or slow them down as needed, depending on what part of the serpentine you are traveling on. You will discover that the better you manage your reins, the less work your feet will need to do.

7. Be careful to not give any extra verbal cues, such as telling your partner what direction to go. You won't have that advantage with your horse, so don't practice it now. Stick to simple cues to move off or stop—sounds or words your horse knows or can easily learn.

8. Don't forget to take your own turn as the horse, blindly navigating the course at your friend's instruction. This will teach you a lot about the importance of giving clear signals and gentle cues.

Once you can guide and be guided around the cones smoothly, you are ready to start work preparing your horse to long-rein.

Desensitizing the Horse to Long–Reins

The sole purpose of this exercise is to see if your horse is comfortable with having long ropes touching and dragging around his legs. When he is (perhaps you already covered it in our *Ground Control* series), you can jump ahead in your training. If not, we have a few methodical steps to introduce and familiarize a horse with long-reins.

EXERCISE

1. Outfit your horse in his halter and a roller, and you'll need your two long-reins. You do not need a bridle or whip for this exercise.

2. Connect a single long-rein directly to the top ring of your roller. You won't run it from the roller to the halter, because at this point, you don't expect control from the rein. All you are looking for is that your horse calmly accepts the long-reins. By attaching a long-rein to your roller's top ring, it allows you the flexibility to practice desensitization from either side without needing to detach, reattach, or readjust anything.

3. For control, attach the other long-rein to your horse's halter as a lead rope. This long-rein will also function as a lunge line later in this lesson.

4. Hold your "lead rope" long-rein in the hand nearest the horse's head. Let the tail trail down from your hand and drag on the ground between your feet, just like when you practiced with your partner in earlier exercises. The long-rein attached to the roller should be held in your other hand (fig. 2.5).

5. You will work to desensitize one side of the horse completely before switching sides, so you will have plenty of practice feeling comfortable with your handling skills before changing anything around. Standing out of kicking range in the center position (to the side opposite the roller—see p. 21) throw the slack loop of rein running between the roller and your hand over the horse's back several times. This action is very similar to one you will use often in long-reining, for example, when you are adjusting the reins to prepare for a direction change. So, your horse needs to be comfortable with it very early in his training. There really is no wrong way to do this

2.5 *The basic setup for the exercise to desensitize your horse to the long-reins. With one long-rein attached to the halter and one attached to the top ring of the roller, you won't have to adjust anything when you switch sides.*

maneuver—just be careful not to slap him with the long-rein, causing pain. The goal is to desensitize him to the sight and feel of long-reins moving around him, showing him there is nothing to fear.

6. As prey animals, horses can be more protective of their fragile belly and legs, so that is why we start with a less defensive place, like the back. Once your horse accepts this, you can gradually get a bit less precise about where the loop of your long-rein touches, brushing his belly and upper legs. If he tenses or acts scared when the long-rein touches any-where, repeat swinging the rope past that area until he calms.

7. One of the areas you will most touch with the long-reins is the hindquarters, so you will need to practice looping the long-rein down over the horse's rump, letting it slide down the hind end to the hocks, and even under the tail. A horse could be surprised by a long-rein that got caught under his tail and spook or bolt, so this is an important part of the desensitization process.

TROUBLESHOOTING

Desensitization

If your horse really has a tough time accepting the long-rein moving near and over him, you might need to go back to just a halter and regular lead rope to introduce this lesson. A lead rope is shorter and more familiar for many trainers, making it easier to begin to introduce these concepts. So, with the lead rope attached to the halter, simply toss the tail of the lead rope over and around your horse, on both sides. The shorter rope and lack of a draping loop and excess tail increases the safety factor as well, giving you the freedom to use the tail of the lead rope all the way down the horse's legs to the hooves, as well as around his forehand and head without fear of tangling. Once he is confident with a rope flicking all over his body, you can return to the exercise with the long-rein and the roller. Often, we find horses will then accept a long-rein's motion around them with little or no reaction.

Advancing the Exercise:
Desensitization Adding Movement and Speed

When you are able to move the long-reins around both sides and all parts of your horse while he stays calm, you are ready to increase difficulty by adding movement and speed. You do this by lungeing the horse in a small circle around you. However, whereas in a traditional lungeing situation you use your voice and whip to start the horse off, in this exercise, you use the long-rein.

EXERCISE

1. To begin, flip the long-rein that is attached to the roller across the horse's back, as before. As when you desensitized his hind end, let it drop around his hindquarters, from the top ring on the roller down the offside, settling just above the hocks before running back to your hand (fig. 2.6). By this time, your horse should not be bothered by any of these actions or placements, but if he is, simply repeat this motion until he calmly accepts it.

2.6 *To advance desensitization of your horse to the long-reins, you will ask for movement in a lungeing type situation. With one long-rein attached to the halter and one attached to the top ring of the roller, let the long-rein attached to the roller drape down the horse's offside and around his hindquarters just above his hocks, running back to your hand.*

2. Once the long-rein is placed around the horse's hindquarters, ask him to move off by pulling on that long-rein firmly. When he steps forward, release the rein pressure and guide him into the circle with your lead.

3. Once he has solidly learned to give to the pressure on his hindquarters going one way at the walk, and he happily moves around with the rein draped just above his hocks, halt, flip the rein around to the other side, reposition yourself, and practice circling the other way. Repeat as needed to put him and you at ease with the lesson.

4. When your horse tolerates walking the circle, ask for a trot by adding pressure to the long-rein draped behind his hindquarters, the same as you did when asking for the walk from a standstill.

5. Practice transitions between walking, trotting, and halts.

TROUBLESHOOTING

Desensitization Adding Movement and Speed

There are a few things to look out for when advancing desensitization to the long-reins in the lunge circle:

- Keep your circles small to increase control. This means you will have long tails to your "lead rope" long-rein and roller long-rein trailing on the ground between your feet. Be aware that they will twist together as you rotate your circle (fig. 2.7). This should not be a problem if you stop periodically to untangle them so they don't trip you.

- Also, at some point the long-rein looped around the hindquarters could drift too high up and under the horse's tail. This is a sensitive spot for many horses, and he might panic. His reaction could be anything

2.7 *It is recommended you stay on a small circle during your advanced desensitization exercises; however, the tails of your long-reins will likely become twisted as you rotate. Stop every now and then to arrange them properly between your legs and out behind you.*

Continued ▶

from simply clamping his tail down to bucking. Regardless, your response should be the same: Use your "lead rope" hand to keep his nose on the circle and release all pressure on the roller long-rein. Tipping his nose toward you prevents him from accidentally striking you with his hind feet if he kicks at the long-rein beneath his tail. And allowing him to keep his feet moving will relax him as he uses up his nervous energy in a constructive way. Eventually, he will release the long-rein on his own from under his tail. Do not pull on it; you'll only aggravate the situation—and possibly escalate the problem—by causing discomfort or pain.

- Sometimes a horse gets nervous when first asked to trot with a long-rein around his hindquarters. He may be calm at a walk, but the faster gait flops the long-rein around more and that might upset him. Use your long-rein attached to the halter to keep his nose on the circle and simply ignore any small outbursts. Just keep his feet on pace. Eventually, he will learn that the long-rein bouncing around is nothing to fear, and he'll settle calmly into the circle.

3

Advancing to a Bit and Two-Rein Work

Now that you and your horse have established some basic skills and communication, it is time to progress to the second part of Level One. In this chapter, you will add a few more pieces of tack: first, the bridle and bit with one rein and later, a second rein.

With young horses, exchanging the halter for a bridle is something new, and allowing them time to familiarize themselves with the new equipment is fine. Once they adjust to carrying the bit with no fuss, the following exercises teach and test responsiveness to rein pressure. While a trained riding horse will not need this adjustment period, he will still benefit from the next steps in Level One. You are primarily teaching him to carry a bit, follow his nose in a circle, and get used to a person working near him.

Remember, Level One is just as much about training the person as the horse. With this in mind, try to find any areas of your own education that need reinforcement. For example, where you stand, rein management, and whip handling aren't important in the first two exercises in this chapter, but by the time you get to the third exercise where the horse circles you with two reins, they become more crucial (fig. 3.1).

3.1 *Level One is mostly about teaching the person instead of the horse. In the first couple of exercises, where you stand, and how you manage the long-reins and handle the whip are less important than the lesson you are teaching the horse. However, as you can see here, once you reach the point where your horse is circling you with two long-reins (see p. 52), you will find you need sharper feel and reflexes, so really begin to focus on improving your form and communication with your horse.*

TROUBLESHOOTING

Position

In later exercises, if you get in front of the horse's roller, you'll have trouble doing them successfully. If this is a rare occurrence, you can just get back into position as quickly as possible before your horse notices. But if you consistently notice an issue with your position in relation to the drive line, this is the time to sharpen your feel. First, review the section in chapter 1 that covers the topic (see p. 19). Then, lunge your horse with a halter and regular lunge line. If you'd like to put a roller on your horse to represent the drive line, that's fine, but don't run your line or long-reins through its rings. The roller should only be a visual marker as you practice finding and maintaining your position.

Lateral Flexion

The first exercise in part of Level One is *Lateral Flexion*: simply bringing the horse's nose around to willingly touch or almost touch his shoulder while his feet remain still. What is the purpose of this, you ask? True, you don't see many driving or riding horses standing around just holding their noses to their shoulders. But it is an important exaggerated step that will serve you well later, no matter what you ultimately intend to do with your horse, and certainly when he's learning to long-rein.

Let's explain. At some point, whether you are weaving through cones or riding around a tree, you will need to pick up your rein to ask your horse to change direction by following his nose (figs. 3.2 A & B). History has taught us if we can guide a horse's nose, we guide his feet. And the rein is our most direct way to communicate when long-reining.

3.2 A & B *Once you have taught your horse to touch his nose to his shoulder with a rein cue, he will find curving around cones or trees in long-reins a snap. Remember, where a horse's nose goes, his feet follow.*

However, the faster your horse's feet go, he'll tend to have a slower, duller reaction to your cues. This is natural, but by knowing about it, you can work around the limitation. You do it by asking for an exaggerated response in this exercise, then making that response an automatic habit. Later, when the pressure is on, you can count on getting the smaller reaction that you actually need. In this instance, you want the horse to learn to tip his nose when you pick up softly on the rein so he will curve left or right with rein pressure. By teaching him at a standstill to dramatically swing his head sideways to his shoulder, you can count on getting the slight tip you need once his feet get moving.

If you have practiced lateral flexion with a halter and lead as we teach in our *Ground Control* series, you should find lateral flexion with a bridle a very simple transition. However, if your horse is unfamiliar with the concept, allow more time for him to grasp the idea.

EXERCISE

1. Start by outfitting your horse with a bridle headstall with snaffle bit (see fig. 1.3, p. 9). If you are standing on the horse's left side, attach a single, standard riding rein or short lead rope to the near bit ring on the bridle. You will stand on one side or the other, next to the horse's rib cage where you can easily reach the withers with your horse-side hand, the entire time, so no sense complicating things with extra rein or rope dragging in your way, especially if your horse shuffles around while he's learning.

2. Flip the tail of your rein or rope up over the horse's back, out of the way, leaving a generous loop of slack from the bit. How much slack? When standing on the left side of the horse, if you can reach with your left hand from where you are standing, grasp the rope, and tip the horse's nose *at least* halfway to his shoulder when you move your left hand toward the horse's withers, you're fine. Remove some of the slack in the rein or rope if the one movement of your hand to the withers doesn't do the job. Here's a tip: The spot to grasp is usually about the halfway point on a regular lead rope, and you can tie a string or stick a piece of tape to mark the spot if it helps. The grasp and flex is essentially the role of the left hand.

3. The right hand rests just behind the withers where it is comfortable for you, gently weighing the excess rein or lead rope in place. This is also a safety measure, because if your horse were to become scared and jerk the lead from your left hand, you could quickly grab it with your right hand to prevent him from escaping.

4. Some horses readily grasp this concept, and when you pull the rein or rope toward the withers, they yield to the pressure. Others feel a bit trapped and may move their feet around or pull against you. If this is the case, maintain your position as best you can, neither loosening nor tightening your pull. Waiting gives the horse time to think his way out, and solutions *he* thinks up on his own usually work better than ones you force on him. If you maintain steady pressure and calmly retain your position, your horse will eventually conclude that the best way to feel comfortable is to put slack in the rope himself.

5. Sometimes a horse will tip his nose but still have his feet moving. In this case, don't release your hold until he has softened his nose and is standing completely still. However, when this happens, you do need to be prepared to drop the rein from your left hand immediately, as if it were suddenly a hot potato. Your quick release might be the most important part to teaching this exercise. The horse doesn't care what response you are looking for, he just wants to understand it as quickly as possible in order to feel comfortable again. If you are quick and consistent when releasing pressure, he will become just as quick and consistent performing good behavior to find the reward. The communication between human and horse that we discussed earlier does matter—your horse can only perform as well as you can communicate.

6. Be sure to practice lateral flexion on both sides of your horse. Set up your reins and hands in a mirror image to the first side. Note: Just because your horse can tip his nose to the left lightning fast, doesn't mean he won't be confused when you ask for it to go to the right. People have the ability to comprehend and apply what they've learned in one situation to a new situation. Horses can't as easily. So, when you start working on a new side of his body, you might as well be teaching a new horse.

One Inside Rein

Once your horse has mastered the idea of Lateral Flexion with a bridle and knows the fundamentals of how to do circles (introduced in the advanced desensitization lesson on p. 35), you have the pieces in place to start actual long-reining. The *One Inside Rein* exercise's purpose is to introduce your horse to the driving equipment and techniques of long-reining. It also sets you up for success, starting out very similarly to a typical lungeing exercise, as well as the advanced desensitization lesson from chapter 2, which lets you practice rein management, the use of a whip, and effective leadership before adding the complication of a second rein. When you do add it, you will be ready.

TROUBLESHOOTING

Following the Nose

Most horses naturally follow their noses, but if your horse has a hard time with it, working in a round pen might shorten the learning curve. The fence's shape encourages him into the correct posture and reinforces him learning to circle around you the right way. Then, when you return to an open space, he will pick up a correct circle by habit.

In this exercise, the horse circles around you, just like the exercise in the previous chapter (see p. 35), but, it teaches two very important new ideas that you will use from here on: *distance* and *speed control*.

EXERCISE

1. To begin, you will need a bridle headstall with a bit and a roller on your horse. Attach one long-rein by running it through your near side bit and connecting the end to the lowest ring on the roller. With the horse's head held naturally, you want the rein to make a straight line from the horse's mouth to the roller so you apply as little leverage as possible to the horse while he learns. The finished long-rein will be shaped roughly like a "V" as it runs from the roller to the bit, then out to your hand. You will need to stand behind the horse's drive line for this lesson (figs. 3.3 A–D). This configuration gives you the most control, which we discuss a bit more in depth later in the *Troubleshooting* sidebar on p. 52.

2. Let's say you plan on circling the horse to the left, initially. You set up the long-rein from the roller through the left snaffle ring as described in Step 1, then step back at least a horse-length away to the side and behind your horse's drive line, feeding rein through your left hand as you go. You want enough slack in the long-rein between the bit and your hand so that you aren't tugging on the horse, but it should be tight enough so there's no

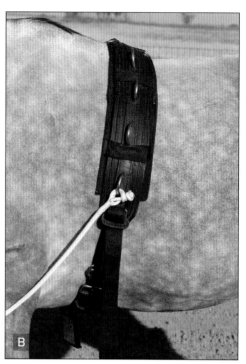

3.3 A–D *To begin the One Inside Rein exercise, thread one long-rein through the near-side ring on the horse's bit (A) and attach it to the lowest ring on the roller (B & C). You and the long-rein will form a "V"-shape when you take your position just behind the drive line (D).*

danger of either of you tripping over the loop. Make sure the long-rein continues to stretch smoothly down from your hand, between your feet, and out behind you.

3. In your right hand, hold your whip, ready to signal the horse to step off. Especially in these first tries, use a carriage whip rather than a lunge whip. You don't want the horse too far from you in case he bolts, so you will keep the circle small. Later, as you both settle into the exercise, you can advance to larger circles, which will require a lunge whip.

4. Tap the whip lightly above the horse's hocks, applying pressure very similarly to when you got the horse comfortable to moving off from a rein cue earlier (p. 36). If needed, ask with a vocal cue and remember to remain consistent with what you use. If your horse is unresponsive, increase whip pressure, tapping as lightly as possible but firmly enough to make your horse move. Ideally, your horse picks up a trot (fig. 3.4). This gait will propel him through the circle without as much danger of a sudden stop as when in the walk. Your horse is also less likely to bolt as he might do if he charged off in a faster canter or lope. If he's not perfect, read on. We cover distance and speed control next.

3.4 *Ideally, your horse picks up a trot as you first ask him to move forward in the* One Inside Rein *exercise. This gait allows the momentum needed to carry him through most lessons, but prevents the possible runaway at higher speeds. If you find your horse moves off too slow or fast, Level One will teach you how to rate him or develop* speed control.

TROUBLESHOOTING

One Inside Rein

- Remember, when your horse travels small circles, such as in the One Inside Rein exercise, your long-rein will bunch and twist under your feet (see fig. 2.7, p. 37). Even though it doesn't have a second long-rein to tangle with, we recommend stopping to straighten it now and then, especially when you are changing direction. It only takes a moment to smooth it back out, and this habit will prevent you from tripping. It also gives you and your horse a bit of a break to catch your breath. This is important for unconditioned horses that aren't used to much exercise.

- We can't stress enough, stay *behind the drive line* to keep your horse moving forward. Driving pressure applied by stepping toward your horse's head or tapping his shoulder with the whip encourages him to change direction, slow down, or stop.

- If you are communicating correctly but your horse isn't understanding, slow your movements down. Once he understands, you can start to speed cues back up. If doing things more slowly isn't helping, don't be afraid to go back to earlier lessons. Get excellent responses there, and you'll be surprised how much better your horse performs the One Inside Rein when you revisit it.

- On the other hand, maybe you have a horse that learns too quickly. Sometimes, he starts anticipating maneuvers like the stop. To fix this, don't stop him in the same place. Switch it up every time, and if he starts to halt without being asked, use your whip just above the hocks to drive him forward.

- If at any time, you feel uncomfortable or like you are losing control, pull on your long-rein. It's set up at this point in a way that gives you the most control, and a pull brings the horse's nose right around to get him stopped. It's the most basic, direct control of the horse's face. In fact, we sometimes call this inside long-rein setup a "safety rein," because that's what it does. It even works when your body position isn't perfect, because you can't overpull the horse with this configuration.

Distance Control

Once you have forward momentum, you must establish direction before your horse drags you off your feet. This means guiding him into a circle with rein pressure to tip his nose. Having taught him Lateral Flexion (see p. 42), he should "give" easily and his body should curve. Once his feet are on the track, relax the pressure. Repeat as needed until he can circle around you by himself.

We are often asked, "How big should the circle be?" As we said earlier, keep it fairly small at first. You want your horse far enough away so he can't kick or strike you if he's feeling playful or scared. That's about a horse-length away. You also want him close enough so if he bolts, you can still maintain some control. That's where the carriage whip is a good measure: when you can't touch him to cue with the whip, he's too far away. If it helps, draw a circle on the ground with powdered chalk to guide you. You want him to begin to curve his body around the path from nose to tail and keep the radius from your feet to his front feet equal no matter where he is in the circle. Correct size and shape circles are important, and now is the time to begin lessons to that end, keeping his attention so he isn't "pulled" toward the gate or another horse.

It is rare that a horse will choose the perfect distance the first time out. That's okay. In the beginning, you want to keep it simple so you can focus on keeping his feet moving around you safely. The whip and the long-rein are how to do this. If your horse is too far away, pull the long-rein to drift him back onto a smaller circle, using Hands Over Fist (p. 18) to gather excess slack that's created. If he is crowding your space, tap his shoulder with the whip in your right hand to drive him away while you feed rein through your left hand. Be aware that pressure in front of the drive line encourages him to change direction.

Once your horse will consistently pick up the circle size you choose, your next step is to intentionally "push him out" onto larger circles and "pull him in" onto smaller circles by spiraling him out or in. You accomplish this exactly the same way you steadied him onto the original path: Loosen the long-rein and wave your whip at his shoulder to encourage him away, and gather the long-rein Hands Over Fist to bring him closer.

Speed Control

As mentioned, ideally your horse will do the One Inside Rein exercise at a trot. Many horses do pick up this gait naturally, and allow you to teach Distance Control first. If yours isn't one of these, don't worry.

When your horse launches off like a rocket, he may settle into a trot on his own after a few playful steps. If he doesn't, lower your whip and pull the long-rein to draw his nose into a smaller circle. It gets progressively harder for horses to travel at high speed as the size of a circle decreases. That is one reason we keep circles small in the beginning. Eventually, you can trust him to maintain gait farther away, but not just yet.

Overly energetic horses are often easier to teach the One Inside Rein exercise. They have enough gas to power around a circle long enough to learn, and you just have to channel that momentum into something productive. Horses that plod off in a walk, on the other hand, require more motivating.

If a horse is in good health and other factors aren't at work (like badly fitted tack, for example), he should be capable of picking up the pace. Otherwise, a low-energy horse will shuffle along in fits and starts, going and stopping, which generally prevents any steady learning. You may need to step up the intensity of your cues until he picks up and maintains the trot. Only then can you continue your lesson.

The Stop

Eventually, you will want to stop your horse. Especially with a high-energy horse, you want him to realize standing at a halt is comfortable, so don't ask anything of him once you get him still. Just let him relax for a bit and catch his breath as a reward. As more energetic horses learn to read you, and realize that standing is pleasant, they will respond sooner.

To initiate the stop, take a step back, remove driving pressure (but stay just behind the drive line so the horse goes forward into the halt), and pull gently on the long-rein. This will straighten the horse's body and slow his feet to a halt. Some horses won't need a rein cue because they are already looking for a good reason to stop. Others will be happily marching along on the circle and will require a firmer hand.

Two Reins Desensitizing Exercise

Once you and your horse are doing well with one long-rein, it's time to add the second while continuing on with the same circle you used in One Inside Rein. Welcome to actual long-reining!

Most of the horses at our clinics are trained riding horses, meaning they are already used to two reins attached to their bit. So, long-reining with two reins isn't a big transition. That's how we are able to introduce this exercise to 15 horses simultaneously. If you have an untrained horse, however, allow him added time to adjust. When working with a young horse, it's best to teach this "mouthing" stage in a round pen by himself.

In the *Two Reins Desensitizing* exercise, you are looking for the horse to continue to give you good lateral bend and adjust to the feel of a second rein, but as with all of Level One, the main focus is *you*. It will take practice for you to learn to handle two reins and a whip simultaneously, so work on this exercise until it not only feels comfortable, it actually feels *natural*.

EXERCISE

1. To begin, your original long-rein will remain attached the same as in the One Inside Rein exercise (see p. 45). Toss the tail of it out of the way on the ground behind you, and about an arm's length away from the bit, drape it over your elbow. This keeps your hands free to attach the second rein, yet allows you to quickly grab it should the horse decide to wander off.

2. As your horse stands quietly, place your coiled second long-rein safely on top of his back. This keeps it within easy reach but out of the way while you walk around the front of the horse to his other side to attach it in the same configuration as the first rein—from roller to bit to hand. Leave the coil on the back of your horse as you return to the other side. Now pick up both reins and allow the opposite rein to slide down around the horse's hindquarters.

3.5 *When first attaching the second rein, manage the reins with one in each hand as Dan is showing here. The goal is to simply have the second rein present, not to use it, so you can familiarize yourself with handling two reins and the whip while providing a low-pressure way to desensitize your horse to the sensation of the second rein draped and bouncing across his hocks.*

3.   Once done, take the center position again (see p. 21), a long-rein in each hand, with your original rein to the inside of the circle (fig. 3.5). Since your reins are set up the same, either side could technically work as the inside, but it is best to use your original rein: For the time being, you want to keep everything as similar to the One Inside Rein exercise as you can, so the addition of the second long-rein is your only new variable.

4.   Then, ask your horse for a lateral bend and guide him into a circle, just as before (fig. 3.6). Ask for forward movement exactly as you did in the One Inside Rein exercise. For now, you just want your horse to realize the second long-rein is there and adjust to the feel of it looped above his hocks. Also, you need time to practice holding the second rein, although you won't actually cue with it yet.

5.   Once you are both ready, be sure to practice in the other direction so your horse gets comfortable with either long-rein being the outside rein (outside the circle). At this point, don't try to use your outside rein to turn your horse and reverse direction. He's not ready for this (and most likely, neither are you). Instead, let him stop, readjust your position, and then send him off in the new direction.

3.6   *Once your two long-reins are run through the bit rings and attached to each side of the roller, ask your horse to move forward on the circle around you. Note that here Swampy's long-reins are attached higher on the roller because of his experience—we recommend you use the lower roller rings when beginning these exercises with your horse.*

TROUBLESHOOTING

The Second Long-Rein

What if you get tangled up or confused when you add a second rein? What if the horse panics when it gets wedged under his tail? Wrecks like this can be very common in the beginning, but you can safely diffuse the situation if you remember to *drop that outside rein like it's a hot potato*.

Although it may seem contradictory, dropping your outside long-rein is often the fastest way to get a horse contained. Sometimes, it's hard to remember because our instinctive reaction is usually to grip harder on the reins. This can really get you hurt if the horse jerks you off your feet or you get tangled up. However, by dropping one long-rein—or both reins—even if your horse completely gets away and runs off to a far corner of the pen, you can always gather him back up and start over.

It's actually amazing how often the horse will just stop by himself when you drop your long-reins. It's because the pressure is gone and you aren't pulling on the reins, aggravating the situation.

This is where the desensitizing exercises we did earlier will help you (see pp. 33 and 35). You will get a sense how your horse reacts to stressful scenarios, like ropes being around his legs or slapping his sides. If he's kicking out at the rope and being very offended during desensitization, you are probably not ready to move on to long-reining.

One Inside Rein, One Direct Rein

Once your horse is accepting the two long-reins, calmly responds to your requests, and you are comfortable with your rein- and whip-handling abilities, you are ready to reconfigure your reins for the *One Inside Rein, One Direct Rein* exercise. The purpose of this lesson is to teach your horse to rely more on rein cues and less on the whip. Increased obedience will improve his transitions and create faster responses. It will also refine his ability to spiral out and in while traveling around you.

EXERCISE

1. To set up, there is only one rein adjustment to make: Your inside rein is connected to the roller, as before, by running through the bit. However, now attach your outside rein *directly to the bit* by threading it through the roller and tying the end of it to the bit. As before, place your long-reins safely out of the way when you move around the horse to adjust your inside and outside reins.

2. Once back in position, place the outside direct rein behind your horse's hindquarters above the hock, as in previous exercises, and ask your horse to move off into a medium-sized circle at the walk (fig. 3.7).

3.7 *In the One Inside Rein, One Direct Rein exercise, run your outside long-rein (outside the circle) through the lowest ring on the roller and attach it directly to the bit. Your inside long-rein remains set up as in previous exercises, and you again ask your horse to move forward onto a circle around you. Here Dan has both reins in one hand as he cues Swampy with the whip to move forward, but at this point, you should continue to use two hands if that is more comfortable for you.*

3. When you have both settled into a comfortable pace, you can start to spiral out by asking him to ease away from you as he circles. Tip the horse's nose with your outside rein to initiate the action. Remember, wherever a horse's nose points, his feet usually follow. Feed your reins out as he circles farther and farther away, continuing to signal with the outside rein

as it slides through your hand. When you near the end of your long-reins, release the pressure on your outside rein to signal to your horse that he should straighten and stop drifting sideways (out). If needed, use slight inside rein pressure to steady him onto the new path.

4. Next, you will begin the other half of the spiral, bringing the horse closer to you. To initiate the inward spiral, use the inside long-rein to direct the horse's nose inward. When the horse is in a small circle, straighten his nose by releasing the pressure on the inside long-rein and using your outside long-rein to steady him on the forward track if needed. Remember, especially as you spiral your horse in with two reins, that the excess tails trailing on the ground between your feet can bunch and tangle. Be aware of this, and take care to step over them. Stop occasionally to untwist them.

TROUBLESHOOTING

The Horse Facing You

Let's address what to do if the horse turns to face you. If you recall, in long-reining, there are three "proper" positions: center, ¾, and directly behind. None of them are *in front* of the drive line.

When using a lunge line or single long-rein, a horse turning to face you isn't a huge problem—you simply push him back out onto the circle. However, when working with two long-reins it can be dangerous when a horse faces you, and you can both get tripped up.

Fix this situation by first dropping both reins—immediately. You don't want one of them getting wedged under your horse's tail or scaring him with pressure in any way. Then, calmly approach him, and grasp both reins in one hand just under his chin. When he is properly contained, you can regather your long-reins and readjust the horse's position.

Advancing the Exercise:

One Inside Rein, One Direct Rein with Transitions and Stops

As your and your horse's skills progress in the One Inside Rein, One Direct Rein exercise, you can seamlessly transition between spiraling out and in without needing to pause to straighten your horse's nose. Instead, simply tip the nose from one direction to the other (out to in and vice versa) to change direction. This is your first step toward true direction changes off rein cues.

Later, you can use this same exercise to transition to teaching gait changes between walk and trot. Speeding up is the same as in previous exercises, with voice cues, the whip, and the pressure of the outside rein above the hocks. You refine dropping to a lower gait by applying direct outside rein pressure, which will slow your horse's feet. When your horse does so, release your rein pressure as a reward. Sometimes, when you give him the release, he will speed right back up. That's okay. Keep slowing and releasing, trusting him to maintain the slower gait on his own. Gradually, he will begin to understand and start to respond correctly.

Eventually, these lessons will help you bring the horse to a stop from rein pressure alone. Refine the slowing cue by holding outside rein pressure until your horse's feet slow all the way to a stop. When you find it easy to transition him from the trot to the walk, for example, it is a simple leap to then go from a walk to a stop. Later, you can ask for a stop from a faster gait with no problem. Once stopped, don't forget to praise your good horse! You want to remind him standing still is comfortable and relaxing.

Two Direct Reins

Much like the last exercise, with *Two Direct Reins*, you will spiral the horse in and out. The only difference is that both reins are now connected directly to the bit, running from your hand through the lowest ring on the roller (fig. 3.8). Unless specifically stated, this is the long-rein setup you will use throughout the rest of the book. It looks like the typical driving reins you might see on a carriage horse, running from the bit through the rings on the roller to your hands.

3.8   *With Two Direct Reins, both long-reins are run through the lowest rings on the roller and attached directly to the bit rings. Here, Dan and Dan spiral their horses in and out on the same circle.*

With the *Two Direct Reins* exercise, you are looking to refine lateral bend to the inside and change directions from rein pressure alone. It also gives you one final lesson to work on the basics of rein-handling before having to move your own feet.

EXERCISE

1. Connect the first long-rein to the bit ring, running it through the lowest ring on the roller. You won't be able to drape it over your arm while you attach the second rein (as you have been doing—see p. 53), due to the new con-figuration. Instead, you can a) flip the tail of the first long-rein up over the horse's hindquarters, letting it fall onto the ground on the opposite side; or b) coil the tail and place it on top of the horse's back, out of the way. The first method leaves the long-rein in a good position for you to collect it to start the exercise once you connect the second long-rein in the same way as the first.

2. Beginning on the side where you attached the second long-rein, gather both reins, letting the first drop down off the horse's hindquarters into place, looped above the hocks. Allow both reins to slide through your hands as you move yourself into the center position (see p. 21).

3. Establish a mid-sized circle at a trot. Review using the inside long-rein to spiral your horse into a smaller circle, and your outside long-rein to increase the size of the circle or to bring him to a stop (figs. 3.9 A & B). Make sure to practice going both ways, stopping between the direction changes to reset.

4. When you and your horse can complete these tests competently, you can try changing directions with rein cues alone. Start at the walk, circling the horse around you.

5. Once the horse is maintaining a steady gait, apply pressure to your outside rein while simultaneously letting the inside rein feed gradually through your hand. Step toward your horse's tail. These motions will shift your horse's weight back onto his hindquarters, letting his front feet step around into the turn. Be careful to not pull so hard on the reins that your

3.9 A & B *Again practice spiraling out and in with your new long-rein setup. Focus on your basic rein- and whip-handling as your horse becomes used to direct contact on both sides of the bit. Here you can see how Dan James demonstrates good rein management of the dragging tails. The excess rein begins to tangle around his feet (A), which happens naturally as the horse circles around you, so he steps forward, as well as turning around (B), which helps the reins find a smoother line behind him, trailing safely out of the way.*

horse loses all forward motion. Forward motion is *key*. If you lose it, it may encourage him to face you, which is the opposite of the desired result. Done correctly, you will spend the entire exercise behind the drive line, with the horse moving away.

6. Bring your horse to a stop, and pointed in the new direction, walk Hands Over Fist (p. 18) until you are in the ¾ position on the new inside of the circle (the opposite side of the horse from where you were just standing), then rub your horse as a reward. As mentioned, you always want to reinforce to your horse that standing still is a comfortable and relaxing default mode. It's usually easier after exercises like this, because he will naturally seek out the rest for a chance to catch his breath.

Beyond the Basics of Rein and Whip Management

To this point, you have worked on rein-handling and some whip-handling. In each of the previous exercises, you have stood relatively still, as the horse circled around you. Practice the lessons up to this point until you are more than proficient with two long-reins and a whip, and your horse is able to navigate each exercise easily.

You may have noticed that we haven't discussed in detail the ins and outs of rein and whip management in Level One, although the section is dedicated to learning the basics. Some things can only be learned by doing, and we have provided all the general guidelines you need to get started. However, there are a few additional tips we can share before you progress to Level Two.

As you get more comfortable using the reins, you may find you can hold them some of the time in one hand, using a second hand only as reinforcement to initiate movements, like changes of direction (figs. 3.10 A–E). This will free your other hand up to hold the whip or untangle reins on the fly during the rest of the maneuver. But, these talents aren't built overnight. Don't try them until you have rein-handling with two hands so automatic that you don't need to look at your hands anymore.

3.10 A–E *As you get more comfortable using the reins, you may find you can hold them some of the time in one hand, as Dan demonstrates in two different ways here: With both long-reins held in the single hand with the thumb on top (A & B), or with one long-rein entering the top of the hand and the other entering the bottom of the hand, so they cross in the palm (C–E). Then, you only need a second hand as reinforcement to initiate movements, like changes of direction. This will free your non-rein hand up to hold the whip or untangle the long-reins on the fly.*

We also haven't discussed whip-handling in detail thus far, and for good reason. The mechanics of how you use one are so individual, although the general rule is that *less is more*, and that applies to both force and frequency. Use the whip as lightly and sparingly as you can to get the response you need.

Before you even go near your horse the first time, you should practice holding and flicking the whip until you are proficient with it. By the time you've reached this stage in Level One, you should be able to read your horse well enough to know when he needs the reinforcement to speed up or change direction that your whip provides.

In the end, it doesn't matter what style you use to handle reins and whip before moving on to Level Two. It only matters that you have learned to signal clearly what you want. That's all your horse cares about.

So far, you may have noticed a pattern of building on each skill in order to get a response from the horse with less work on your part. Exaggerated hand movements become smaller cues, subtle enough to be virtually invisible to bystanders. When you and your horse can do the exercises in this chapter with that kind of refinement, you are ready to progress. You are prepared to start combining your newly minted rein- and whip-handling skills and actually drive your horse somewhere. Flip the page to chapter 4 to learn how.

4

Beyond Circles — Advanced Level One Exercises

Welcome to long-reining—in the most classic sense! In this chapter you will add *actual driving* to the rein-handling lessons you've already conquered. Most horses will seamlessly transition from traveling circles to traveling forward, as the motion is only a slight change for them. As with all of Level One, this chapter is for *you*. In it, you will now move your own feet—walking and jogging to keep up with your horse.

Until now, with the horse standing or circling in each of the previous exercises, you have remained relatively still and focused on using your hands. Many of our students find their own footwork a bit tricky at first, because you are not only using long-reins...and you are not only walking—you must do both at the same time. However, don't worry. By the time you finish the three exercises in this chapter, you will have it down. You will also be ready to begin serious training with your horse in Level Two.

One note before we get started: The more efficient you are with your hands, the less you will have to move your feet to keep yourself in position. Any holes in your rein-management education will show up right away in the first lesson. However, view that as a good thing. It's a built-in self-check. Just go back to earlier exercises, work on anything glaring, then return to this chapter.

Now, let's begin the first lesson.

Walking Down the Arena

In the *Walking Down the Arena* exercise, the goal is simple; teach your horse to go forward with you following. To help, you'll need some cones (fig. 4.1).

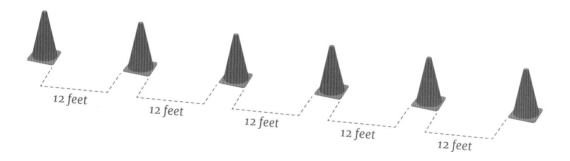

12 feet   12 feet   12 feet   12 feet   12 feet

4.1 *Create a straight line of six cones in the middle of your arena or the pasture where you are long-reining. There should be approximately 12 feet (3 meters) between them, allowing enough space for your horse to weave between one pair and turn in time to come through the next pair.*

Think back to the Long-Reining a Person exercise (see p. 27), when you had a friend pretend to be the horse and you wove her in and out of cones. That, essentially, is this exercise, although now you will be long-reining your horse, *and* we're going to take it a step further and advance the exercise with a few simple position changes.

You will reinforce your rein-handling skills while your horse learns to travel a path other than that of a circle. In the beginning, most horses find it a bit difficult to understand the concept of a straight line, but they already know how to change direction and to step sideways and forward at the same time (from your spiraling in and out exercises). So, we fill the gap with this exercise: Walking Down the Arena teaches a rapid series of direction changes, keeping in mind that you will eventually straighten these sideways motions into forward movement.

A note of encouragement here: We find that as a student improves her skills, her horse automatically improves too. Chances are, you won't be perfect on the first try, so keep practicing!

EXERCISE

1. To start, begin at one end of the line of cones, in the *directly behind* position, about a horse-length away from your horse (remember this is a safety measure in case your horse decides to kick).

2. Proceed forward, weaving your horse through the cones exactly as you did with your friend in Long-Reining a Person (figs. 4.2 A & B). Use soft, clear pressure on each long-rein to cue your horse which direction to go. As you begin to move remember: You may need to slow or speed your feet in order to stay in position; and the better you get with your hands, the less you'll have to do with your feet.

3. If you find you need a bit more control when starting this exercise, try stepping your horse out into wide turns to each side as you approach and go around each cone. This will slow the maneuver down, giving you both time to think through each phase.

4.2 A & B *Begin to weave down the line of cones in the directly behind position, practicing your cues for turning as well as moving your feet and keeping the long-reins trailing neatly between your legs and out behind you. The line of cones Dan is using here has the cones about 12 feet (3 meters) apart.*

Advancing the Exercise
Walking Down the Arena ¾ Position

Once you have your horse consistently and smoothly weaving through the cones, you are ready to up the challenge.

EXERCISE

1. Step into the ¾ position beside the horse and to one side of the cones. Lengthen your long-reins so you are standing an increased distance away from the horse (but not so far that you sacrifice control).

2. See if you can stay to that side of the cones while you weave your horse through them. Ideally, your feet walk a straight line parallel to the cones, while your hands instruct the horse (figs. 4.3 A–C).

3. When you can do this exercise consistently walking on one side, switch sides.

4.3 A–C *Step up the challenge of weaving your horse through cones by stepping to the ¾ position and allowing more distance between you and your horse (that is, lengthening your long-reins). This lets you walk a straight line off to the side, while you move your horse through the cones.*

Advancing the Exercise

Walking Down the Arena in the Cones

In this most advanced version of the Walking Down the Arena exercise, you will stand in line with the cones and walk as straight as you can down this centerline, weaving the horse back and forth in front of you.

EXERCISE

1. Begin by asking your horse to step to one side just as if you were sending him off into one of the earlier versions of this exercise.

2. Now, rather than weaving your horse in and out of *every* cone, count four strides, then signal him to turn back across the centerline (figs. 4.4 A–H). These four strides will bring him back to the centerline roughly every other cone or so, depending on his stride length. For this drill, however, the cones are really merely a marker to keep your feet traveling straight.

3. The important part to focus on with your horse is the number of steps he's taking. It's easiest to count them if you pick a front leg, and count its motion. As your horse travels back across the centerline in front of you, your count restarts. Four strides, then ask him to turn back to the line of cones. The reason for precisely four strides is that it's enough time and space to allow you to work on speed control and accuracy, but not so many strides that your horse feels tempted to run away. However, don't forget good rein management and contact, in case he does decide to "leave." Some horses don't need much encouragement to run off, although at this point your horse should be pretty tuned in and locked onto you.

4. Although you are using the cones just as straight-line markers in this phase of Walking Down the Arena, your horse should have enough self-awareness to step fluidly around them as he crosses the centerline, instead of knocking them over. You should too! Keep working at it until you both have your feet coordinated.

4.4 A–H   *In the most advanced version of the Walking Down the Arena exercise, you remain in a straight line with the cones as you weave your horse back and forth, every four strides, in front of you. Note that your goal is to remain in as straight a line as possible, although you may need to step to one side or the other to accommodate your horse's turn, as you can see Dan does in this series. At this stage, you and your horse should complete this exercise at the walk. Dan and Swampy demonstrate it here at the trot only after perfecting their communication at the slower, more manageable gait. Dan also wants Swampy to keep his face more consistently on the vertical.*

Trainer Changing Positions

Once you can walk a straight line and move the horse back and forth in front of you, it's time to swap these roles. In the *Trainer Changing Positions* exercise, the *horse* is the one walking a straight line, and you alternate between walking in the ¾ position and directly behind him. The goal is to practice and perfect your body-position changes and awareness in relation to your horse.

This exercise is simple, but very important for later exercises. You will probably find it harder than it seems. You can use the line of cones again, or a long fence or wall can serve to guide your horse along. For the purposes of our example, we will assume a fence.

EXERCISE

1. Begin behind your horse, and ask him to follow the fence line at a walk. This will be his role for the entire exercise, and most horses readily do so, plodding along half asleep before you finish learning the lesson. If he has trouble with staying on the fence, take the time to practice keeping him there until he understands.

2. Now, maintaining a safe horse-length distance from your horse, quicken your step sideways and forward until you are in the ¾ position (figs. 4.5 A & B). You know you are there when you are halfway between the roller and his tail. As you step, you will simultaneously need to lengthen your outside long-rein and gather your inside long-rein's slack.

3. Once you step to the ¾ position, continue to walk your horse forward as you slow your feet and glide back behind his tail in the directly behind position. Lengthen your inside long-rein and shorten the outside long-rein smoothly until they are even.

4. As your horse walks a straight line, continue to practice transitioning between the two positions, until it is effortless.

4.5 A & B   *At the standstill, Dan demonstrates moving from directly behind Swampy (A) to the ¾ position (B) in preparation for the Trainer Changing Positions exercise. Note how he simultaneously lengthened the outside rein and gathered the inside rein evenly as he stepped to position. This prevents any unintended tension on either side of the horse's mouth.*

Lateral Yield

Our last Level One exercise is the *Lateral Yield*. In this instance, it doesn't involve touching a horse's nose to his shoulder (see the earlier exercise on p. 42), but rather is meant to teach a horse to step his feet sideways away from you, similar to a side-pass and very much like a leg-yield when you are riding. A two-part exercise, you will be very familiar with the Lateral Yield if you have gone through our *Ground Control* series. If you haven't, don't worry. You should have mastered all the rein- and whip-handling skills you need to teach this exercise to your horse by now.

In this exercise, you start your horse down the fence or wall, exactly as in the Trainer Changing Positions lesson. Here too, you will toggle between walking directly behind or at a ¾-angle; however, unlike the Trainer Changing Positions exercise, you will travel a straight path parallel to the fence while *pushing* and *releasing* your horse's hip into position. Let's explain. For this example, the fence is on your right.

EXERCISE

1. Begin in the directly behind position, and ask your horse to simply walk forward along the fence, with you following him.

2. To begin the Lateral Yield, you want the horse's nose to stay next to the fence while his left hip swings away from the fence toward the inside of the arena or pasture (fig. 4.6). To do this, loosen your left long-rein and gather your right at the same time. This pressure will tip his nose to the wall and his momentum and the presence of the outside rein will carry his body into the correct position. His change in position also changes yours—because you continue to walk in a straight line, you are no longer directly behind him, you are now in the ¾ position. You will need to reinforce and continue the forward-and-sideways movement by tapping his hip with the whip.

4.6 *To begin the Lateral Yield exercise, keep your feet moving forward on as straight a line as possible while you give with your inside long-rein and add pressure to your outside long-rein. This will tip your horse's nose toward the fence (to the right of Dan in this photo) and naturally move his hindquarters toward the inside. You will need to tap the outside hip with the whip to keep forward motion, as the momentum will carry the horse into the right position as well as changing Dan's from directly behind to more of a ¾ position than we see here.*

3. At first, you only want a step or two of Lateral Yield, where the horse moves sideways and forward at the same time. Then, drop the whip back and even up the contact in your reins to allow your horse to relax back into walking straight along the fence, with you directly behind him. This

is enough to practice in the beginning. You want your horse to transition back and forth from straight to Lateral Yield until he is no longer worried about it and is very consistent with his response.

4. When he is ready to move on, add the number of steps gradually. Ask for three, then four, and so on, until you can have him yield along the entire length of the fence. Obviously, if your fence is longer than an arena, take that into consideration—no sense making him yield the length of the property. Although, he'd be very good at it if he could!

What you have here is the horse walking forward as much or more than sideways. You expect his hip to lag a bit behind his nose, and that's okay. You are just trying to teach him to move away from a driving pressure, which directly translates to leg cues under saddle.

However, with practice and refinement, you can certainly get pickier on alignment of the nose and hip, and teach your horse to travel a true side-pass down the fence. It just takes work encouraging his hip to keep up, while not losing the momentum he needs to prevent his feet from stopping. This is hard to do, and a little bit of forward motion helps horses from getting stuck or confused.

For your purposes here, though, you are looking to build to a *three-track movement* instead. Your horse's shoulder will be a little ahead of his hip, allowing for that forward movement. You will be in your ¾ position. It is easy to tell in this exercise when you are in the proper position. If you look down at your horse's feet, you will be able to see three of them. His far front will be hidden mostly from your view by the near hind. Also, as he steps away, you can see three lines of hoof prints in the dirt (where the term "three-track movement" comes from). This is because his two aligned hooves are traveling the same track, in the same exact direction.

Advancing the Exercise

Lateral Yield Front End

The second variation of the Lateral Yield exercise has the horse shift his front end away from the fence, rather than his hip.

EXERCISE

1. Begin as in the Lateral Yield in the directly behind position, and ask your horse to simply walk forward along the fence, with you following him.

2. To begin the *Lateral Yield Front End*, you want the horse's nose and shoulders to tip away from the fence while his hindquarters stay along the fence (fig. 4.7). To do this when the fence is on your left, loosen your left long-rein and gather your right at the same time. This pressure will tip the horse's nose away from the fence or wall, and again, just as before, his momentum and the presence of the right rein on the right hip will carry his body into

4.7 *Dan walks in a straight line down the fence while Swampy travels in front of him in a three-track movement: the Lateral Yield Front End exercise.*

the correct position, changing your position, too. You will need to reinforce and continue the forward-and-sideways movement by tapping his hip with the whip.

Advancing the Exercise:

Lateral Yield and Changing Direction

You need to teach your horse to Lateral Yield from both sides, so when he is doing well one way, it's time to switch sides. You have two methods to reverse direction:

Method One

First, you can use the horse's body position to help the transition by turning him *into the fence* (fig. 4.8).

1. If you are doing the Lateral Yield exercise with his nose already tipped toward the fence and his hip to the inside, just increase whip pressure on the fence side to push his hip on around.

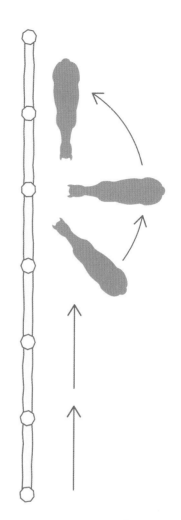

4.8 *Method One for changing direction when practicing the Lateral Yield along the fence or wall: turning into the fence.*

2. The fence will stop your horse in front, and he will swing his hind end around into position, ready to travel the other way along the fence.

The only downside to this method is that you have to be quick on your feet to keep up with the horse's hip.

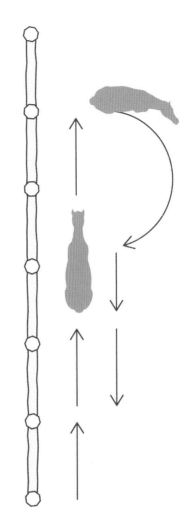

Method Two

So, that is why there is a second method: turning *away from the fence* (fig. 4.9). Here, rather than the horse's hip moving so much, it's his shoulders. You need more rein-handling skill and less fancy footwork.

1. To begin, let the horse relax into following straight along the fence.

2. Then, tip his nose away from the fence and take him in a half-circle back to the fence, where he will be facing the new direction.

Whichever method you use is up to you, and we encourage you to try and master both techniques.

Eventually, with practice, you can ask your horse for Lateral Yields without the help of the fence or wall. He should understand the cues to shape his body enough so that he doesn't need a physical barrier to hold him in place (fig. 4.10).

4.9 *Method Two for changing direction when practicing the Lateral Yield along the fence or wall: the half-turn away from the fence.*

TROUBLESHOOTING

Lateral Yields

There are a couple things that confused horses commonly do when learning to do *Lateral Yields*, but if you are prepared, they are pretty easy fixes.

- The first is "sticky" feet. This means you are yielding the horse sideways and he stops. Usually, this is a result of an overly ambitious trainer. Remember, you are literally teaching *one step at a time*. Why would you think that if your horse can hesitantly take one step, he should be able to do five?

  The trick is to stop before you feel him try to quit. If you think you can get him to give you three steps, stop at two. By rewarding him for two good steps, instead of shoving him through that last one, you will find he sees the experience as a positive one and might just give you that extra step on his own next time. You will also find that stopping while you are ahead will make "sticky feet" disappear all on their own. And you will progress to longer periods of *Lateral Yield* sooner, with much less effort.

- The other common problem teaching *Lateral Yield* is when the horse drifts away from the fence during the yield. Rather than chasing him all over, staying in the ¾ position, don't be afraid to step back directly behind him and push him back to the fence. Then, you can ask him to step back to where he is supposed to be in the Lateral Yield. It's better for you to step out of position, fix the problem, and get back than to stay rigidly in place where you can't correct it.

4.10 *When your horse can consistently and confidently perform lateral exercises near the fence, you can try them without the aid of a barrier, as Dan is doing here. Just imagine a fence on one side or other of your line of travel, and you'll see how your cues remain the same depending on whether you want the hips or the forehand to move to the inside of your track.*

Level One Wrap-Up

At this point, you have done all the Level One exercises. Now is a good time to self-test to see if you are ready to move on to Level Two. Remember, Level One was all about preparing *you*, and laying the groundwork education for your horse. If you don't have it down, you do not need to go any further until you do.

1. With light rein cues can you guide your horse into circles in both directions?

2. Will he halt from voice and rein willingly and immediately?

3. Can you change directions easily, whether it is around cones, against the fence, or just in the open?

4. Does your horse spiral in and out, as well as yield down the fence with ease?

If the answer to all these is yes, then turn the page. You are ready to begin schooling your horse in earnest. Compared to what you had to learn in Level One, your horse's lessons were relatively easy. Most riding horses, which is what most of our students bring to us in clinics, will have many of these lessons in their toolkit already or will find them simple to accomplish. So, when *you* are ready to advance, your horse should be ready and waiting.

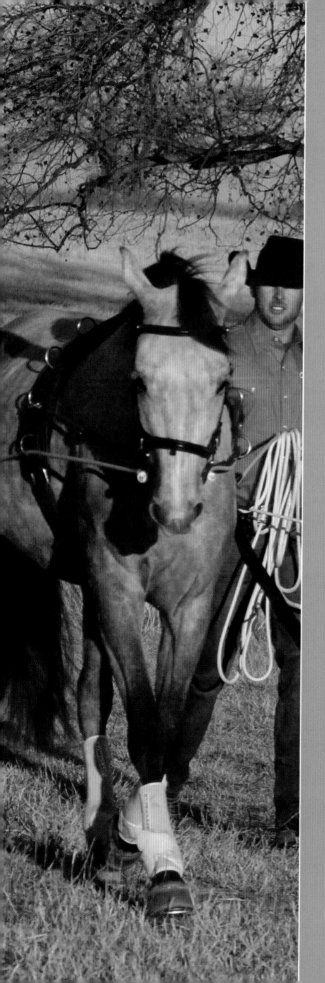

5

Transitioning to Teaching the Horse

Welcome to Level Two! In this chapter, we will advance what we covered in Level One, first by adding speed to the maneuvers, then by adding new ones. In this level, you move from *teaching yourself* to *teaching your horse*.

We advise that you work through Level Two with a quiet, well-mannered horse before you try to re-educate a horse with training or behavior problems. When you are learning long-reining, it's just like riding for the first time. It's better to learn with an easier horse that lets you focus on your own education. If a non-horse person comes to your house and asks to ride, you don't put her on the unbroke horse or the one that likes to buck, do you? No, you walk past those two in the pasture and pull out the gentle horse that will make her first ride an enjoyable one.

Helping problem horses work through their troubles, either on the ground or under saddle, requires a certain amount of confidence in your methods. This only comes with practice and experience. That's why we ask that you wait to retrain difficult cases. However, our typical clinic student ought to be able to coach a friendly youngster or average saddle-broke horse that just needs some polishing through Level Two, just fine.

One note on colts: If you take a colt through the long-reining exercises we've already covered and reach Level Two, when you do finally hop on and ride, your youngster will be much more advanced than he would be without his long-reining education. He will already be able to stick to a circle. He will be able to do three-track maneuvers. He will be familiar with having something strapped to his back and working off rein cues. All you are introducing is a rider, so it should be a relatively simple transition.

Warm-Up

Let's ease your horse into the first Level Two lesson with a quick review of Level One. If you have any trouble with the prerequisite warm-up exercises, go back and practice them as needed until you and your horse are solidly performing them. By this time, they should be easy, and you should recognize each exercise from the Level One wrap-up.

1. To start, ask your horse to pick up a simple circle with you a horse-length away, using two direct reins, in the ¾ position. Begin with a walk and then transition smoothly to a trot (fig. 5.1).

2. Once your horse has found rhythm, point him into a spiral, using Hands Over Fist techniques to reel him in and out (see p. 18).

3. If your horse is doing well at this point, steer him into a change of direction (see p. 77) and practice the same exercises going the other way. You are looking for the horse to willingly keep the forward momentum up, or lower his energy, as you ask and while you maintain steady contact and provide clear cues.

4. The final test is to try Lateral Yields in both directions, looking for crisp, three-track movements. You should also be aware of your body position and be able to adjust as needed to keep your horse moving correctly.

5.1 *Quality circles are paramount from here on out. If you spot any weaknesses shaping the horse into an effortless, round one, it's time to troubleshoot. You both must have the muscle-memory in place to do calm, perfect circles at any time. Dan trots Swampy in a circle using two direct reins as part of a warm-up before starting Level Two exercises.*

If you and your horse can perform all these competently—staying soft, calm and responsive throughout—you are warmed up and ready to try something new. However, if you get stuck with any exercise, don't be afraid to step back, get your horse's confidence up, and then build back to this point again.

Roundness and Softness

With this exercise, you are ready to start having training goals for your horse rather than yourself. You have a sound foundation with long-reining techniques and can move your horse forward and side to side as needed. The goal for the *Roundness and Softness* exercise is to refine these movements, teaching your horse to round his body and accept the bit softly.

About Circles

You'll recall that we've been a bit picky about how the horse travels on circles from the beginning. We've worked hard to curve his body around the path from nose to tail, keeping the radius from your feet to his front feet equal no matter where he is in the circle. Correct size and shape circles are important, and all the exercises you've done so far should have built your horse to a point where he travels the circle around you without wavering, or being pulled toward the gate or another horse.

You wouldn't allow your horse to go wherever he wanted if you were riding, and you shouldn't allow it in your long-reining either, since these lessons set the stage for under-saddle work. Before you focus on roundness and softness, you need to get his attention on *you*—not every outside distraction. Don't do anything further in Level Two until your horse has One Inside Rein circles down (see p. 45). You are just asking for trouble if you do. If you are working with an unbroke horse, you will be amazed how much making sure he knows how to stick to a circle will help you.

Your goal here is to introduce speed, and this exercise teaches your horse to carry himself at speed obediently and confidently. In the Roundness and Softness exercise, you will canter (or lope) for the first time in your long-reining training. (Note: For the purposes of this book, we will use the term *canter* throughout to mean the three-beat gait just faster than a trot—simply because it is the one we grew up using in Australia.)

You only need one long-rein and a lunge whip for this exercise. Remember, we try to keep everything as simple as possible in the learning phase, for both you and your horse. A second long-rein won't be used at all in this exercise, anyway, so you might as well set it aside for the time being.

EXERCISE

1. Attach the long-rein by running it through the bit and connecting it to the roller, exactly as you initially did in the One Inside Rein exercise in Level One (see p. 45). If you recall, with this setup, it is almost impossible to over-pull on your horse's mouth. As with all our exercises so far, use a lower ring on your roller to run the rein through, to give the gentlest signals.

2. To begin, ask your horse to move onto a trot circle (fig. 5.2). A large-sized diameter is best because it frees the horse up to transition most easily into a canter. Small circles can bind a horse up and be too physically taxing to canter around. We will discuss this more in depth in the next exercise.

5.2 *Begin the Roundness and Softness exercise with one long-rein set up the same as for the One Inside Rein exercise (see p. 45), and move your horse out onto a circle at the trot. Spiral him out until he is on a large-diameter circle that will allow room for him to canter—but don't give him so much rein he loses track of what he's doing and who he should be focused on (you).*

However, don't give your horse the entire length of the long-rein because with too much distance he might be tempted to let his mind wander away from you...and with added speed, his feet could follow. For now, send your horse out onto a circle about a half-a-long-rein away at an easy trot, focusing on keeping a quality lateral curve of his body as he tracks around.

3. By this time, your horse should carry himself with correct posture: nose tipped into the circle, rib cage pushed out, tail curved inward, mirroring the nose and completing the half-moon shape of his body. It is important that your horse can give you this "roundness" of body and soft, cadenced gait in a circle at the trot before asking for the canter.

4. When you do ask for the canter, keep light contact on the long-rein and whip, ready to adjust as needed to maintain your horse's forward motion. With a voice command and wave of the whip in the air above his hocks, ask for the transition. At this point, do not look for your horse to travel much distance at the canter. You are only looking for a stride or two, and then go ahead and let him relax back down into the trot. Your horse may take the wrong lead, but don't be concerned about that either. All you are concerned with right now is that he is trying and learning to make that transition back and forth between trotting and cantering.

5. Practice this speed control, going faster and slower several times during one round of the circle.

6. As your horse masters this, quickly and obediently responding to your request for speed, you can slowly increase the number of strides you ask him to canter. Your goal is to eventually maintain the canter for a full circle. When your horse is trained enough to do this, he is capable of going further, if needed. When first teaching this lesson, you will need to walk to keep up with your horse as his circles wobble around. As he learns to steady his circles at the canter, you will be able to move your feet less and less. Ultimately, you will be able to keep your feet still. Instead of walking to keep up, you'll be able to swivel on a heel in place to maintain position with your circling horse.

7. Don't forget that whatever you teach on one side of your horse, you must repeat on the other. Generally, horses will be more comfortable going one way than another, much like right-handed or left-handed people write. Keep at it until he is equally at ease traveling both ways.

Advancing the Exercise

Roundness and Softness—One Inside Rein, One Direct Rein

When your horse is circling well, just as in the previous level, it is time to step up to the One Inside Rein, One Direct Rein exercise. If you recall, this exercise uses the Hands over Fist technique to spiral the horse around you. However, in this level, you will perfect it at the trot and try it at the canter. Don't be surprised if your horse seems to forget how to listen when you first try spiraling at the canter. Often, sending a horse away from you at a faster gait dulls his responses, and in these early stages, sometimes he'll feel like he's running wild and free.

EXERCISE

1. Set up two long-reins as you did for the One Inside Rein, One Direct Rein exercise in Level One (see p. 55).

2. Ask your horse to trot the circle, and spiral him in and out a couple of times (fig. 5.3).

3. When he is settled and ready on a larger-diameter circle, ask for the canter.

4. With your inside long-rein, ask the horse's nose to start the spiral in. This small cue is often enough to focus his attention on the task at hand. Once

5.3 *Previously, you taught the horse to travel on a circle, and you've now practiced cantering with One Inside Rein. In this more advanced stage of the Roundness and Softness exercise, you advance the lesson by changing the long-rein setup to One Inside Rein, One Direct Rein and asking your horse to spiral into smaller and larger circles. As always, start with the trot, and when the horse has nice shape and good forward movement and is focused on you, as Swampy is demonstrating here, you are ready to ask for the transition to the canter.*

on track, let him play a stride or two if he wants, and see if he settles into cantering smoothly around you on his own.

5. If he decides to run away instead of taking the cue to spiral, don't panic. Use more pressure on your inside long-rein to tip his nose to the circle and a light outside long-rein cue to help steady his pace. If he rates back too much and slows to a trot or stops, that's okay. Send him off again onto the circle and then start the spiral again.

6. Practice in both directions.

TROUBLESHOOTING

Roundness and Softness

With this, and any of the following exercises, weak areas in your training will only be magnified and worsened with the addition of speed. Avoid potential wrecks that will set back your training by allowing plenty of practice at the trot before asking for a canter.

- If your horse is struggling at the trot to maintain correct form and rhythm as he travels, reinforce lateral bend by stepping back and bringing his nose slightly more toward you. Remember to release rein pressure as soon as his nose is where you need it, and don't forget to wave your whip at his hip while you are applying pressure to keep his feet moving forward. If he gets confused and thinks you are asking for a stop with your rein cue, it's no problem: Just send him back out onto the circle and restart the exercise. Your horse will eventually learn to relax into the new shape, his body following his nose in a curve around the circle. When he can do this comfortably and consistently, he is ready to try cantering.

- Another issue you can run into during this exercise is the horse only trotting faster when you ask for the canter. This is very common with lazier-tempered horses. If yours doesn't respond promptly to your request to canter off as asked, you will need to apply increasing pressure until you get the response you are looking for. If a voice command and wave of the whip in the air above his hocks aren't enough, you will need to tap the whip lightly on his hindquarters. Increase contact gradually until he moves off in the faster gait. If you are consistent and clear with your signals, he will learn quickly. Then, each time you ask for a canter departure afterward will be easier.

- Sometimes, horses travel a different gait with their front legs than their back ones. It is common—especially with lower energy horses—to look like they are slowly loping along, when really only their hind legs are. If you look closely, the front feet are trotting. You can easily tell because the horse won't be traveling a nice three-beat gait, with one front leg touching the ground at the same time as the opposite hind. Fix this issue by asking for more speed, just for a stride or two. Livening up his feet will automatically force him to be snappier and more correct with his movement. Then, when you allow him to relax back down into a slower canter, he should be more precise.

- If your horse is finding it difficult to speed up, the size of the circle may be your root problem. Send him out onto a larger circle. Sometimes, horses will trot in front because they need extra room to stretch their legs properly. This is common in longer legged breeds, like Thoroughbreds. In this case, a bigger circle may be all he needs to clean up his gait.

Advancing the Exercise

Roundness and Softness—Two Direct Reins

As when progressing through the stages in Level One, the next step is to attach both long-reins directly to the bit, and run them through the lower rings on the roller to your hands (see p. 58).

EXERCISE

1. As in the last exercise, use the outside long-rein to guide your horse into a circle around you.

2. Pick up a trot and spiral in and out smoothly several times (figs. 5.4 A & B).

3. Progress to a canter and then into the spiral again.

4. Once your horse is proficient spiraling in and out one way at the trot and canter, don't forget to go the other.

5.4 A & B   Roundness and Softness *is further advanced by trotting and cantering spirals with Two Direct Reins, as Dan and Swampy are doing here. You can see how Dan is using the inside long-rein to tip Swampy's nose in, guiding him inward onto circles of decreasing size (A). Once Swampy is a whip-length away, Dan will begin spiraling back out (B). Note the Lungie Bungie on Swampy in these photos is discussed in more detail in chapter 7, p. 117.*

TROUBLESHOOTING

Roundness and Softness—Two Direct Reins

- Remember when you spiral your horse to you, don't force him in too close to you. An established horse will have the training and muscle tone to hold the gait in a tight circle, but a novice will find it too mentally confusing and physically exhausting (fig. 5.5).

5.5 *Swampy has the experience and conditioning to maintain his shape and control on a very small circle around Dan; however, we don't recommend circles this small for most horses and handlers at this stage of training.*

- If your horse continues to be tempted to run away when you spiral him out, take note of the distance where the problem starts. Usually, it is at the same place each time. Set yourself up for success and make this "problem point" the farthest you feed out the line. Take him right to the edge of where the bad behavior begins, and then reel him back in to you. Eventually, he will canter as solidly around you at that distance as he does when closer in to you. Then, you can try a small test. Push him out a bit farther away. If he tolerates the new distance, well, great! Next time you spiral him out, give him more rein. But if not, make this your new boundary. Keep working until you can easily spiral him in and out the full length of your long-reins.

The Back-Up

Now is as good a time as any to introduce backing up on the long-reins. If you've got a good stop, the back-up is only adding one more ingredient. By this point, you have established good communication with your horse and developed your long-reining skills enough to maintain his respect. Because we use backing up so much under saddle, it's important to introduce it as early as you can.

The reason we leave out backing up until Level Two is because the horse can use it as an evasive measure, putting you in front of the *drive line* and out of control. If you don't have your long-reining skills solid enough to allow you to move quickly to correct position, he can learn to use the back-up against you, and you won't be ready for it. This issue usually starts with your horse shuffling his feet backward when you ask for a stop. You may think he's an overachiever and doing well; however, be careful to watch this habit. It can actually be him anticipating another maneuver and preparing an evasion. You'd like him to wait for you to tell him the next move and have confidence going *forward*. By the time you reach Level Two, he should be listening well enough and have that confidence. With those pieces in place, he won't get stuck and shuffle away.

Prerequisite to the Long-Rein Back-Up

Before you ask your horse to back up with long-reins, he should be able to do it with a halter and lead. It is surprising how many people we see at clinics who can't do this, and it can be a big deal. While some horses won't have any issue diving right into backing with long-reins, others really do need this foundation step. Ex-racehorses are a prime example. A horse off the track might not have had any experience backing away from a handler—ever. It's just not generally a requirement for racehorses. They are bred and trained with forward motion in mind.

Dan James had extensive experience working with racehorses during his time in Japan, and he noticed that even when given the opportunity, racehorses will not back up during the course of their day at pasture. He's seen cornered Thoroughbreds try to jump tall fences rather than back up a couple of steps to get out of a jam. Their mindset is so focused on going *forward* they don't even consider the alternative, and that is only reinforced by the fact they are only encouraged to go forward in training.

Sometimes, when you first apply contact to the bit to ask for a back-up, horses unfamiliar with the cue and movement don't understand the concept. A halter and lead simplifies introducing the idea of softening and yielding their feet away from backward pressure. For in-depth instruction on teaching this lesson with a halter and lead, refer to our *Ground Control* series.

Backing Up with Long-Reins

When you ask the horse to back up in the long-reins, it doesn't mean 50 steps. Someday you can do this, but in the beginning, if you can get a couple of obedient steps backward, you are doing well. You can always build from there.

EXERCISE

1. Ironically, a good back-up starts with good forward motion. With two long-reins directly attached to the bit, establish a basic walk circle, with you in the ¾ position.

2. Once your horse is moving with cadence, prepare for the back-up by stepping directly behind the horse's tail a safe distance away. Pull back evenly on both reins until your horse stops and takes a step back.

3. *As soon* as your horse shifts his weight backward, throw slack in your reins immediately—it should be as if you will be burned if you apply pressure one second more. Immediate reward of correct behavior like this makes your horse snappier about backing up because he will seek this relief from pressure in the future (fig. 5.6).

4. Give your horse time to settle into a halt, both before and after asking for the back-up. Be patient. You want to allow him time to process the exercise, teaching him to not worry about the back-up. It will also prevent him anticipating immediately taking off again, and by default, reinforces him waiting for your cues.

5.6 *As soon as you horse begins to shift his weight backward after you ask for the back-up, release the pressure on the reins as Dan is doing here. Aim to get a step or two at first, and build from there.*

5. As he becomes comfortable with moving backward, gradually increase the number of steps you ask for. You will find you can use increasingly lighter cues to initiate the back-up. Eventually, this work will help you refine your horse's headset and body collection: You will be able to maintain gentle, continuous contact with the horse's mouth during forward motion, which will allow you to feel and signal communication faster with your horse. You'll find he will begin to shift more of his weight to his hindquarters, ready for you to send him off into any direction. The more you practice backing up, the better his collection will become, and the more his muscles will develop properly. These results will help with any exercise, especially down the line, when he needs to balance a rider.

6. As you practice, you will gradually be able to switch to backing up from the ¾ position. When you horse is able to respond promptly and correctly with you slightly off to the side rather than directly behind, you are ready to advance to the next exercise.

6

Combining Speed, Direction Change, and Spirals

Now that you can move your horse's feet front, back, left, and right on command—at the speed you choose—you are ready to refine these maneuvers by using several lessons in combination. There is nothing "new" to teach in this section. You are simply looking to develop lightness and obedience before moving on to something more challenging.

Lightness and Obedience

EXERCISE

1. Begin with two reins connected directly to the bit. Ask your horse to walk around you in a circle.

2. Spiral your horse out at a walk. Once he is at least a horse-length away, raise your whip to signal for a trot. Remember to watch that you don't forget basic safety, like staying aware of tangling long-reins between your feet.

3. After your horse settles into the gait, try a series of *direction changes*, looking for smooth transitions from your horse. If he has any trouble, keep alternating course until your horse can effort-lessly tip his nose away from you and pivot his front around to pick up the new circle. Forward move-ment is key to changing direction. Lose momentum, and his feet will shut down. That's why it is so important to establish a good trot to carry your horse through the turn (figs. 6.1 A–C).

4. Your position at this point will also change. By this time, your horse should understand maintaining a circle on his own and be read-

6.1 A–C *The exercises in this chapter refine and build on previous lessons, such as controlled circles at speed (A), spirals in and out (B), and changes of direction (C).*

ing your body language quite well. So, you don't have to be as careful about staying in the ¾ position. Now that your horse's education is well under way, it will help you to step closer to the *drive line*. This will give you greater control of distance, allowing you to put pressure on his shoulder when necessary.

5. You can also work on building your horse's frame and muscles by asking for his hind legs to reach farther underneath him. Touch his inside hip with your whip to lengthen the stride. You are not looking for greater speed so much as larger steps.

Serpentine

At this point, you have developed a high level of communication with your horse. With a two-loop pattern, the *Serpentine* exercise works to sharpen the accuracy you have in directing his feet and awareness of where you are standing in relation to him. Combined with speed control and changes of direction, it will test everything you have learned so far. None of these skills are new, but the way they are put together is.

The Serpentine's purpose is, like all the earlier exercises, to improve the horse's body position. However, it advances things because we have markers (cones) set up, which force you to be very aware of your own position in order to keep the horse moving correctly. You used cones before in Level One (see p. 66), although you will set them up a bit differently in the Serpentine. You will need six cones to be placed as pairs in a row (fig. 6.2). The two cones in each pair need to be placed far enough apart for your horse to be easily driven between them, but close enough together so that he will need to think about them as he steps through.

6.2   *In preparation for the Serpentine exercise, set up six cones in aligned pairs with enough space for your horse to move between them on the long-reins.*

EXERCISE

1. For this exercise, your horse will again be outfitted in the standard setup with two long-reins attached directly to the bit.

2. You can use your horse to help determine how far apart to place each of your three pairs of cones. Arbitrarily place two sets in a row with a "gap" between them. (We'll adjust this gap next.) The two pairs of cones should be directly opposite each other.

3. Standing centered in the "gap" between your two pairs of cones, circle your horse in a walk or trot around you, near the end of your long-reins. You should be able to reach him with the longe whip if a cue is needed, but the size of the circle should allow your horse plenty of room to canter if you wish. Your horse's path should take him directly through the center of each pair of cones without him breaking stride or needing to step to either side to avoid stumbling over a cone.

4. With your distance between pairs determined, choose one set to be your middle pair of cones, and set up a third pair in line with and the same distance from your first two.

5. Send your horse back onto a circle the same size as before, letting his path tell you if you need to adjust the final pair of cones. When you are finished your test, his hoofprints should form two loops in the dirt that look something like the number "8," touching each other only in between the center pair of cones.

6. Now to begin the real exercise: Stand to one side or the other of the center pair of cones and ask your horse to pick up a circle at the walk or trot. You should be at the ¾ position.

7. So far, you and your horse should have found this exercise easy, but give him a moment to settle into the circle anyway. When he does, let him continue on until he reaches the center pair of cones and stop him in between them. Now, you will prepare to switch circles. We are often asked why we don't just steer our horse into a change of direction to pick up the second loop of the eight. At this stage, horses are often quite capable of this, but

we find it is better to break things down and take them slow. Many horses aren't bothered by the new setup, but others can be overwhelmed at first if you push too hard. So, try to give them every opportunity to ease into this new idea. It also takes some speedy footwork on the handler's part to change positions between circles on the fly. For this reason, it is best to get a feel for where you need to be by doing each circle separately. Then, when you have to run faster to keep up and quickly find your position, you will know exactly where to go without too much thought.

8. So for now, once your horse is stopped in the center, and step yourself from one side of him to the other, where you will take up the other ¾ position and guide him on to his new path, around you in the opposite direction.

9. If you both handle this well, maybe you can try a change of direction back again as soon as you reach the center pair of cones again. Or, if you have been walking, try it at a trot. Get creative, and incorporate previous exercises into the Serpentine to keep things fun for you and your horse.

Coordination

In our clinics, we often use an example from when we were kids that is familiar to our audiences in Australia and America: Can you pat your head with one hand while rubbing your belly with the other?

Most can do this easily enough. But, can you alternate which hand does which task? How about while hopping on one foot or skipping? That's the level of coordination you can work up to with long-reining.

We find people start struggling with coordination as soon as they start incorporating more than two things. This is when it gets confusing. And, that's why in Level One, we spend so much time building your coordination with simple, individual exercises. From the Serpentine exercise on, you are building on those concepts you learned in Level One and combining them together. If you get to this point in Level Two and your rein management and body position are poor, it shows.

TROUBLESHOOTING

Rein Management in the Serpentine

We spent a considerable amount of time building rein management skills in Level One of this long-reining program. The Serpentine is the first exercise that demonstrates *why*. For the first time, you are combining more than one maneuver in quick succession, and if you don't have good long-reining habits, you can get hurt.

Say the horse is moving away from you on the circle: You should slow your body down so you don't get in front of him. But, as he comes past you in preparation for the change of direction, you will need to speed up to stay behind him. In this exercise, you can easily get dragged off your feet if you get to the end of your long-reins and are in the wrong place or moving at the wrong speed. For the same reasons, you can also get stuck in front of your horse, with too much slack long-rein trailing on the ground.

Extra rein may not seem as big of a problem as getting dragged off your feet because you suddenly hit the end of the line, but if your long-reins are draped so low they're touching the ground, you're setting yourself up for trouble. Your horse can step over a rein, tangling himself up. Or, if he suddenly takes off, you can get whiplash because he will have plenty of slack to pick up speed before you feel the impact. That's why it's so important that you maintain *light contact* with the mouth. It was a good idea in previous exercises, but it is paramount from here on out.

Unless you're looking for collection, you always want a light contact in long-reining. Light contact can also mean a loose rein, not just constant tension on the bit. Too much tension will just make him dull to your rein commands.

Whether your light contact's loose rein is an inch of slack or a foot, this sometimes comes down to eye appeal. However, with an inch of slack, you can pick up quickly to make adjustments. With a foot of rein, there is not just a delay when you are driving, there is a leverage effect. The farther back you are, the more you have to use Hands Over Fist to find a position where you can control the horse if you need to ask for a new maneuver or if he spooks.

Often in clinics, we find that students who are too far away from their horse—with too much slack in their reins—forget Hands Over Fist and panic when they need to cue their horse quickly or he misbehaves. Instead of Hands Over Fist, they opt for what Dan Steers dubbed "Chicken Wingin.'" This is where they pull back, elbows flying to find contact, reminiscent of a flustered hen (fig. 6.3 A). We tell them that if they get a hand past their hip, they're Chicken Wingin', and to remember to get that long-rein gathered up in front of them. But that's sometimes hard to remember.

Think of it this way: If you're riding, you don't guide your horse with your hands behind you—it's awkward and you have no control. It's the same from the ground, except all of your rein-management coordination mishaps are magnified and exaggerated (figs. 6.3 B & C). This is because your long-reins are so much longer and, as your primary form of communication with a horse, will show up in his reactions much more than regular riding reins, for example.

6.3 A *"Chicken Wingin'" is often a result of poor rein management and panic combined. It reminds us of a flustered hen (A).*

Continued ▶

6.3 B & C *You also shouldn't be in a position where you are communicating with overly exaggerated movements, way up high, down low, or out to the side (B). The goal when long-reining is small movements of the hands for rein cues, with elbows by the sides and hands near the belt buckle (C).*

Rein management is so important throughout the exercises, but particularly in the Serpentine. Depending on where your horse is in the Serpentine, you are speeding up or slowing down to maintain position and this makes Chicken Wingin' especially easy to do. This is different from most of the earlier exercises where you simply follow along at one speed. If you discover that you are a Chicken Winger, just keep practicing proper techniques. It won't take too long to improve—our clinic students usually return home recovered from the affliction.

In the *Serpentine*, you will need most coordination when your horse is between the center pair of cones, as this is where you will ask for the change of direction that puts your horse on a completely different circle. Unlike other changes of direction, where the horse simply turns around and goes on while you stand fairly still, changing circles requires you to step from one side of the center cones to the other to maintain ¾ position inside each circle. To do this, you need to have rein and whip cues that are automatic and be able to use your hands independently of each other to keep your horse on track. At the same time, you will speed up your feet to catch up to your horse, keeping you behind his roller and preventing your reins from becoming a tangled mess. But, don't worry, if you get in a jam, just stop and reset. Or, if you feel a wreck is imminent, drop those long-reins until you can safely regain control.

Remember, it's far better to have to catch a loose horse and stay safe than it is to get hurt because you bobbled with coordination.

Intermediate Lateral Movement

In Level One, we introduced lateral movement in the Lateral Yield exercise (p. 73) by walking the horse down a fence or wall and then moving his hips or forehand over to a slight angle (a three-track exercise). At that phase, we were mostly looking for forward movement, with *just a bit* of sideways step. Your goal was not only to heighten your horse's ability to listen to you, but also to prepare him for under-saddle work, like stepping sideways, which comes in handy for things like opening a gate, moving out of a passing rider's way on a narrow path, and smoothly avoiding obstacles.

It is time to build on that. At this level, you are not going to ask for more speed. Instead, you are advancing the exercise by asking for greater sideways action and precision. You will keep the horse's nose to the fence in the beginning, but bring him off the barrier as his confidence grows.

EXERCISE

1. To start, have your horse pick up a walk circle away from the fence or wall.
    Roll the longe whip's string, tucking it out of the way or use a carriage whip
    for this exercise. You need to stay in quite close for *Intermediate Lateral
    Movement*, and a shorter whip is perfect for this task. Your horse should be
    circling close enough to you so that you can touch him with the tip of your
    whip if needed.

2. Once your horse is smoothly walking on the circle, push him closer toward
    the fence or wall until he is circling right next to it.

3. As he comes around to approach the fence and you are ready to initiate
    your Intermediate Lateral Movement, tip his nose to the fence (with your
    fence-side rein) while you step to the ¾ position on the opposite side. The
    momentum of the circle and the fence-side rein should propel his hip over
    and send him fluidly down the fence into the exercise (fig. 6.4).

6.4   *The Lateral Movement exercise
is a continuation of the Lateral Yield,
which you learned in Level One. Again
you ask the horse to tip his nose
toward the fence and bring his hip off
the straight track he is walking as the
fence serve as a guide for his basic
path. Now, though, you will ask for a
greater degree of angle to his body.*

4. Tap his fence-side hip if needed to keep him in position. It's been a while
    since he's practiced the Lateral Yield exercise so he may need time to
    refresh himself on the technique. Give him time to do that, not asking for
    too much angle or many steps at first.

5. Then, let him relax into simply following the fence at a walk.

6. Repeat the circle near the fence to again practice Lateral Movement. When your horse can hold a slight yield for several strides, try angling his hip a bit more toward the center of the arena, until you work up to a three-track movement.

7. With practice, your horse can step sideways down the fence with little to no forward motion at all—his body aligned perpendicular to the fence from nose to tail, or close to it. When he can accomplish it consistently and effortlessly, it's time to ask for something more.

TROUBLESHOOTING

Intermediate Lateral Movement

With a fence (and you) to physically "hold" the horse, and a good foundation of yielding to the bit to prevent him from bolting forward, the most common trouble you'll find when walking a lateral movement down the fence is for your horse to try backing away. Generally, just like at Level One, this happens as soon as you try to push his hip farther than he is comfortable.

If he drifts away from the fence at any point, take your position directly behind to push him back up where he should be for the exercise. Then step back to the ¾ position and continue the exercise without making a big fuss about it. Horses will typically stop trying to shuffle away as their confidence builds. If he does more than drift and really comes off the fence (whirls away or takes large steps toward the center of the arena or pasture), you will need to respond with an equal reaction. At this point, simply pushing him back to the fence a step or two won't fix things. Instead, use his momentum to circle him back around to the fence where you can reset the exercise.

Continued ▶

Since you are asking him to keep his nose near the fence, you don't want anywhere else to feel comfortable. Really hustle his feet to get him back there, especially the farther off course he goes. Then stop and let him relax once he is in place. Soon, he will be seeking for a fence to put his nose next to like a magnet! Later, when you ask for his nose to be placed elsewhere, he will learn that comfort is actually found anywhere you ask him to be. But in the beginning, let the fence be a good visual aid to help you teach the concept.

Advancing the Exercise:
Intermediate Lateral Movement—Tail to the Fence

Your horse is ready to try the next phase of the Intermediate Lateral Movement exercise when he can step sideways down the fence with little to no forward motion at all.

EXERCISE

1. Start by setting up the exercise exactly the same by circling your horse next to the fence.

2. Then, when he approaches the fence, instead of tipping his *nose* to the fence, use your reins to support and maintain his body's curve toward the center of the arena as you tap his hip with the whip and ask him to walk sideways off the circle path and down the fence with his *tail* to the fence (fig. 6.5). It can be tricky at first, since many horses want to "leak" toward the middle of the arena, but use your long-reins to block the drift and your whip to continue driving him sideways. He will get it with practice, and the better you can coordinate your signals, the faster he will learn.

6.5 *Once your horse can do the Lateral Movement exercise with his nose to the fence without forward motion at all, just sideways (a true side-pass), it is time to try the exercise with his tail to the fence. As before, start by asking for just a little angle and a few steps and progress toward a three-track movement.*

Advancing the Exercise:

Intermediate Lateral Movement— Off the Fence

Eventually, you work up to doing the Lateral Movement exercise without the support of the fence, which you can begin by intentionally easing him away from it. Gradually, start him off the circle and into the exercise farther and farther away, until the fence has no bearing on his ability to step laterally in a straight line (figs. 6.6 A & B). It sounds simple, but will take time and patience. At any time, step closer to the fence again, reestablishing good form. Then you can try again. With all phases of Intermediate Lateral Movement, you are looking for your horse to respond to rein and whip cues quietly and correctly.

At this point, your horse is pretty far along with long-reining, and if you are working with a youngster, you could start under-saddle work now. Before you do—or before you move on to Level Three, which will prepare your horse's mind and muscles for some more challenging riding maneuvers—try the following Wrap-Up. As in Level One, this self-check will tell you whether you and your horse have the green light to go on.

6.6 A & B *Gradually work on the exercise further and further away from the fence, until your horse can come off the circle and into either Lateral Movement in the middle of your arena or pasture. Here, Dan demonstrates stepping out of the introductory circle and into the Intermediate Lateral Movement—Tail to the Fence exercise.*

Level Two Wrap-Up

Keeping your horse soft and calm, in this Wrap-Up do a quick review of all the Level Two exercises. Since many of them build on each other, it shouldn't take long.

1. Pick up a circle, emphasizing forward movement with a whip cue to the horse's inside hip. Transition through the walk, trot, and canter. Spiral in and out at all three gaits. Halt and change direction often and sporadically, to keep your horse on his toes. Back him up.

2. Off the circle, do a Lateral Movement without using the fence for support. When you are in the ¾ position, you should clearly be able to see his three-track movement.

If you are successful in all of these, you are ready for Level Three. Turn the page to begin our most sophisticated long-reining exercises.

7

Refining Long-Reining

Welcome to Level Three—the most advanced of our long-reining exercises! In the following lessons you will begin to refine control and work toward collection by building on previous exercises. To do this properly will require a high level of communication and trust between you and your horse, which you have spent the first two levels cultivating.

This final section should really read "Level Three and Beyond" because we will set you up through the end of the book to carry on with your long-reining if you wish (figs 7.1 A–C). And, you really can take long-reining very far—think of the Lipizzaner stallions of the esteemed Spanish Riding School in Vienna, Austria. They entertain thousands every year by showcasing long-reining training techniques used throughout history as preparation for battle.

Starting with this chapter, all the lessons are focused on teaching *the horse*. You should have a good understanding of where to be when, and how to efficiently use the reins and whip—all the basics. If so, you have all the tools you need to start educating your horse in some pretty impressive, as well as useful, maneuvers.

7.1 A–C *Level Three is where you begin to refine collection and control with your horse by building on previous exercises. Here you see Dan and Swampy demonstrating the communication they have cultivated over years of working on long-reining exercises together: From lateral work to more advanced in-hand maneuvers, the relationship you build with your horse on the ground with the long-reins can help develop solid, forward, willing performance.*

Starting under Saddle

For most of our students, the goal is to start or re-start their horses under saddle, using long-reining to teach each lesson before attempting it astride. We often get asked if it is a requirement that someone works all the way through all the long-reining levels before climbing on. Well, the short answer is no...but it's not a terrible idea!

The long answer is a bit more complicated. It really requires being honest with yourself about your horsemanship abilities, your horse's capabilities, and your time constraints. Both mentally and physically, you must be able to do the exercises in this book, and you must have the time to train them consistently. Once you do that, you can better assess when under-saddle lessons can begin. Patience is a virtue, and going too slowly in training won't tend to get you hurt, whereas going too fast certainly can.

Our rule of thumb is that if you are an "average hand" in starting untrained horses, you can go ahead and start your horse under saddle after Level Two. If you're an exceptional talent and not worried about the first ride, you might get by riding after Level One. Be prepared for some fireworks though, if you're trying it that soon.

When we say you can start your horse under saddle at a certain point, it doesn't mean you should jump right into the equivalent of Level Two or Three long-reining exercises under saddle. It means you will get on the horse and go back to the very first lesson of Level One. Changing your position changes everything and you need to make the transition as easy as possible by asking very simple tasks of your horse. Once your horse is comfortable with that, you can alternate lesson focus between under-saddle work and Level Three long-reining to keep things fresh and interesting.

Each added long-reining level makes that first ride and every one after that much easier. It also condenses your early saddle-training time because your horse will already know the lesson. You just have to teach him to do them with you sitting on his back instead of standing on the ground:

- Level One gives you the bare minimum of control. It gets your horse to be obedient enough so that you can avoid many problems progressing through later long-reining or riding sessions.

- Level Two builds on that framework with exercises that start to get more fun and discipline-specific. It is the level that also really builds your horse's communication with and confidence in you.

- Level Three refines things further and is when you grow your horse's physical and mental development for bigger maneuvers. In this level, you're asking for things like flying lead changes, which will be integral in many events, such as dressage or reining.

What Level Three Produces

All the exercises in Level Three create a control and flexibility in the horse that has proven beneficial to equestrians of all types since horsemanship began. Whatever direction you and your horse are headed, long-reining can set the foundation to get you there. From headlines to the front lines, advanced long-reining has long proven a good way to introduce concepts to the horse that will be carried over to under-saddle or driving work.

Although long-reining in Level Three is primarily educating the horse, there are still things it can teach the person. You have the advantage to actually watch a horse's movements from the ground, which gives you the best vantage to see how he handles himself. With time, you will also learn how your horse is best presented, like positioning his head carriage to the most pleasing and functional placing for his individual conformation.

The development of the horse through the previous levels is what makes work in a "frame" a possibility now. It takes progressive strengthening and suppling of the horse's body, as well as teaching him to be receptive to your cues while maintaining his forward energy. You cannot skip steps to get here—everything we've worked on prior is what prepared you for this stage of training. If the horse is not forward, is not already soft in your hands, then trying to create a certain headset will backfire. What happens with the horse's head and neck is ultimately about what's happening with his hind end. The exercises we will work on in the pages ahead will begin to package that energy coming from behind.

What you will learn in Level Three are important accomplishments that can come only through observation and lots of practice.

Watching Movements from the Ground

It's really hard to feel an action for the first time. Say you ride your horse to a stop, and I ask you if his feet stopped square and balanced; you'd have to look to see if one is sticking out wildly. But if you're long-reining your horse to a stop and I ask the same question, you can answer me in a split second because you can see what's going on with his feet.

The same principle applies to seeing things like footfall during a canter or other movements. You can see things from the ground you just can't from the saddle. Then, when you are sitting on the horse, you have an idea of what is happening under you. I'm not saying if you long-rein you'll suddenly have the feel of an Olympian, but at least it's a transition and a starting place.

Head Carriage and Frame

Head and neck position and how your horse carries himself is another big benefit to the exercises in Level Three. Early in his training career, Dan James put all his horses in the same frame under saddle, meaning he asked them to carry their heads in approximately the same place, with a little variation for conformation. That is, until one day, when respected fellow Australian clinician Ian Francis rode by him.

"He told me let a little rein go there, take a little rein in there. He kept changing it until he said, 'There. Feel that? That's where *this* horse looks the best.'"

Where a horse "looks best" is within the scope of his anatomical capabilities, so he can perform willingly and soundly with his face on or just in front of the vertical.

"In my mind, I had a general idea of where my horse's head should be, but he judged the horse's conformation to create a better look. With that simple change, he made my horse actually look *better* than what the horse's conformation actually was."

Now, we discuss ideal head carriage in our long-reining and riding clinics. However, we do keep in mind that it is a personal thing that depends on a lot of factors, like discipline. While Western horses tend to drop their heads lower naturally, in English riding, heads are usually carried higher. Neither is wrong if not exaggerated. We've seen horses perform the exact same maneuvers very well with many different head positions (fig. 7.2). That's why we don't have a one-size-fits-all head carriage and frame for everyone in our clinics.

7.2   *We don't believe there is one ideal head carriage or frame for all horses—instead, the position of the head and neck should suit the horse's conformation and level of training and conditioning, as well as discipline.*

What Age Can a Horse Begin Level Three?

Level Three long-reining needs to be reserved for horses that are three years old and up. Younger horses don't have the physical strength or coordination to perform most of the exercises you will be asking of them from here on, and you need to give them time to mature and build fitness.

However, it takes considerable time to properly work through the first two levels, so age and maturity shouldn't be a limiting issue for most horses. Rome wasn't built in a day, and neither are equine educations. You have to teach your horse each lesson, repeat as needed to commit to memory, and review to test or refresh his recall. So, when he finally has the knowledge and fitness to continue on, he will usually be old enough to do so.

The step from Level One to Level Two is pretty rapid. Remember, we're were working on the person as much as the horse in those early lessons, so it's not that mentally or physically taxing for an average, friendly, willing horse to zip through them. However, plan on Level Two taking at least a year. That is where the real work begins, and you will probably need that long for your horse to be able to consistently perform those exercises.

Re-Educating Problem Horses

Many of our students come to us with a horse that has at least one behavioral issue. If that's your case, your own training (meaning *your* capability with the long-reins, whip, position, and long-reining exercises) should be through at least Level Two before you try to re-educate your problem horse. As we mentioned at the beginning of the book, it's hard enough learning while simultaneously training a calm, trusting horse. It's incredibly difficult to learn yourself while working with a troubled one. The more troubled the horse, the more solid your long-reining skills should be.

When you are long-reining for the first time, it's just like riding for the first time—it's foreign. From knowing where to stand to long-rein management, everything feels awkward, and you have to think about every tiny decision. That's why it's better to first practice on an easier horse. Give you and your problem horse every chance to succeed. Stack the deck in your favor if at all possible, and learn long-reining on a more willing equine partner first. Once you are proficient with the basics, you can focus on training a problem horse, instead of yourself.

Warm-Up

Let's say you and your horse have aced the pre-flight check list from the Level Two Wrap-Up (p. 108), and are ready to move on to Level Three. As in both of the earlier levels, you'll begin with a warm-up that consists of skills your horse is already good at performing. This firm foundation is especially important at this level because you will soon be asking some pretty difficult things of your horse. You want him to be mentally and physically prepared to accept the challenge. There is nothing new in the warm-up, except the purpose. You and your horse should have these movements down automatically.

The reason for doing them now isn't to teach, but as a confirmation that your long-reining skills and his mind and body are ready to take on more demanding exercises.

1. Start with a simple circle, walking your horse around you with two long-reins directly connected to the bit and a lunge whip. As he loosens up and settles into the task, send him out away from you on larger and larger circles until you are close to holding the ends of your reins. Try trotting, then a soft canter. Halt and back him up. Change directions and work him the other way.

2. After he proves that he's listening to your requests and responding well, review more advanced lessons. Spiral in and out. Practice Lateral Yields down the fence, both types and both directions, and then again without using the fence for support.

3. If he is doing well in the warm-up so far, ask your horse to lengthen his stride without necessarily moving out faster. This will allow an energetic horse time to burn off a bit of excess energy and encourage a laid back horse to stretch his muscles and tendons before the hard work begins. A human athlete needs time to "get in the zone" before practice or a big game and so does your horse.

How do you know when he's found that sweet spot and is ready to move on? You are looking for your horse to willingly obey your requests as you transition him through gaits and changes of directions, quietly responding as you ask. If he is running away, grabbing the bit and pulling the reins through your hands, or if he has sticky feet and refuses to maintain gait, you should stay right here, reviewing the first two levels until those exercises are routine.

Once you have confidence in the warm-up and feel your horse is mentally and physically ready, you can start to educate him. The first step is teaching basic collection and extension. You've already eased into the concept by asking for the stride to shorten or lengthen at times, both in this warm-up and in earlier levels. Now, let's investigate collection and extension more in depth.

Collection and Extension

Each horse has a natural stride length in every gait. He is capable of shortening (collection) or lengthening (extension) it as needed to fit everyday situations he will encounter in the pasture. Horses come hardwired at birth with this ability to collect and extend each gait. All we are teaching in Level Three is that we'd like them to do this on command. As communication and the horse's fitness grow, you can start to ask him to collect or extend for longer amounts of time.

Why is this level of communication and physical training necessary? Take collection, which allows a horse to change direction in an instant. It doesn't matter if he's cutting a cow, performing in a circus, or passaging down the centerline, an instant ability to collect is important to effectively do them all.

Using the Lungie Bungie

There is a new piece of tack we use throughout all of the following exercises in Level Three. We introduced the Lungie Bungie to you briefly at the beginning of the book (see p. 13), and now will explain it to you in depth (figs. 7.3 A–C). We find this piece of equipment is an invaluable training aid to encourage collection through the combination of forward movement into the light contact it provides. Collection physically takes longer to develop than extension. Extension *stretches* and *loosens* the muscles, while collection *strengthens* and *grows* them. Much like a bodybuilder works his arms and legs to be able to lift a heavy weight, a horse must prepare his neck and back muscles to maintain a frame and head carriage and hold the rider, as well as balance his own weight, properly. The Lungie Bungie helps ensure he does that. Note that you can certainly complete the exercises in Level Three without a Lungie Bungie; however, we do not recommend the use of side-reins in its place.

The Lungie Bungie consists of a short, inelastic strap that connects from the bit, on both sides, to a small ring just behind the horse's chin, much like a loose curb strap. Then, two elastic bungie cords split from the ring and snap onto each side of the roller. Placement of the two snaps should be approximately midway down your roller. Adjust your Lungie Bungie length on each side so that there is a light connection with your horse's mouth. This will start to encourage your horse to hold his head where it suits his conformation

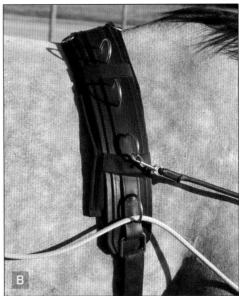

7.3 A–C   *The Lungie Bungie has two short elastic reins that run from a ring be-*
hind the bit to the roller. Developed by professional event riders in conjunction
with a top tack manufacturer, we find it to be an invaluable training aid to encour-
age the horse to carry his head and neck in a frame suitable for his conformation
and level of training. The Lungie Bungie attaches to the bit via a short strap, much
like a curb strap (A) and to the roller (B) and can be adjusted so there is light con-
nection to the horse's mouth (C). Proper fit provides a gentle cue, and it is better
to start overly loose than scare your horse with too much pressure.

best. Too loose, and the horse can poke his face out without any contact at all, which does nothing to train his muscles. Too tight, and you will make him uncomfortable and quickly fatigued. Too much contact can also scare some horses because they will feel trapped. It is better to err on the side of too loose, because you can always adjust it tighter without much fuss, but once you scare your horse with a piece of tack, it takes that much longer to make him comfortable with it once it's on correctly.

Proper fit should give your horse a gentle cue, releasing the pressure when he is in the proper position. If he chooses to "root" his nose forward and down, which is typical in the beginning, it provides a non-threatening pressure until he yields. Most horses will pull against this new pressure until they learn to find relief through giving to it. We find the Lungie Bungie helps during this process in two ways:

- First, the horse pulls against himself, not you. This saves your energy and keeps him from resenting you as the one annoying him with pressure. It also makes it easier for you to regain control if he decides to fight or panic.

- Second, rather than a hard-and-fast rope knot, such as what is on the long-reins, elastic is forgiving. It expands and contracts. This protects your horse's mouth from sudden jerks and is mentally an easier cue for him to accept. He is allowed to pull away from the pressure, but it gets increasingly more uncomfortable as he does so. This freedom still teaches the concept but helps a lot of horses not feel so trapped.

Using Long-Reins with the Lungie Bungie

What about the long-reins while you are using the lungie bungie? We use them at the same time throughout Level Three. Attach your long-reins to the bit above your Lungie Bungie strap. Then, run them back and through the roller rings just below where the Lungie Bungie clips to the roller on each side of your horse. The two actually work well together. The Lungie Bungie works on contact and head and neck position, which frees the reins up to direct the horse's feet.

Once your horse has quieted his mouth and accepts the Lungie Bungie as just another piece of tack, you can ask him to move off around you in a basic circle.

You aren't as concerned about training anything specific just yet, except getting him used to wearing the Lungie Bungie while in motion. So, the familiar, elementary circle at a walk or trot is best. Choose the gait at which your horse is most comfortable. It's best not to canter, however, because with that much speed, he might get too excited and try to leave you.

When your horse can do all the warm-up exercises from p. 115 with the Lungie Bungie, you are ready to move on (figs. 7.4 A–C). However, the more familiar and comfortable he is before moving on, the better. At this point, he should be gaining confidence with the contact and taking the first steps toward collection, more effortlessly gathering his feet underneath himself instead of sprawling them out and stumbling over them everywhere. This automatically means he will learn to simultaneously lift his back and hold his face on the vertical. True collection, where his weight shifts from being heavy on the forehand to evenly balanced, meaning he is physically positioned to launch into any maneuver you need, will come over time as his body grows stronger and his mind more accepting.

7.4 A–C *Accustom your horse to the feel of all the equipment by going through the warm-up from the beginning of this chapter, including* Lateral Yields *(A), simple changes of direction (B), and spiraling in and out on a circle (C).*

Next Steps

Once your horse is secure in the first two levels, you have begun to think about the concepts of extension and collection, and he's comfortable wearing the Lungie Bungie, it's time to move on. Turn the page to dive deeper into Level Three.

8

Speed Control, Transitions, and Obstacles

You may not realize it, but you have eased your horse into the idea of collection and extension in many of the previous chapters. Through our *Speed Control within the Gait, Controlled Transitions,* and *Obstacle Exercise* series, you will continue to build on that training. *Speed Control* and *Transitions* are all about collection in a very hands-on way, while *Obstacles* can teach both collection and extension very passively, letting the horse discover things for himself as he finds his way through a course.

This order of lessons is a nice way to set up for the rest of Level Three. It starts with some very targeted instruction, then ends with a laid-back form of coaching. The mental and physical break of traveling over obstacles is a good breather between the first two exercises and the next chapter, which is also all about being very precise and collected.

Speed Control within the Gait

We will begin with the *Speed Control within the Gait* exercise. It is actually made up of an integrated group of lessons that investigate the fine balance of forward motion with collection, so we will cover them all together. As discussed before, extension doesn't take as much training of the mind or body for the horse to master, while collection can be much more taxing and harder to learn. So, that is why most of our upcoming exercises will focus on *strengthening*.

Note that when you ask for collection in these Speed Control lessons, you never want to rate your horse back so much that he loses forward motion and a soft, round frame. This will be key. The goal is to keep him engaged and moving, not overwhelmed and shutting down. Light hands and not being afraid to review earlier lessons will make that happen.

EXERCISE

1. Begin with a familiar circle, using the Lungie Bungie, two long-reins attached directly to the bit, roller, and a longe whip. Take the center position, which you will use throughout this series of exercises.

2. After your horse has established the circle, spiral him in and out at a walk, trot, and canter. Only when he is listening well do you ask for speed control, or collection.

3. Initiate collection when the horse is out on a large circle. Try it first at a walk.

4. With your outside rein, instruct your horse to stay on the circle instead of drifting toward you in a spiral. Once he does and is moving out in a fluid, forward walk, use slight pressure on both reins to ask for a shorter stride *without* breaking gait. The goal is for him to shorten for three strides then

release the pressure on the long-reins and allow him to extend back to his neutral length of stride (fig. 8.1).

5. Repeat in both directions.

8.1 *Once your horse is traveling well on the walk circle around you, ask him to collect for three strides, then release the pressure on the long-reins and encourage him to move out in his neutral stride. I want Swampy to move nice and forward into the contact, bringing his face onto the vertical.*

Advancing the Exercise:

Speed Control within the Gait—Canter

As with all exercises, the more solid your horse is with something going slowly, the better he will be at it when you add speed to the mix, so spend as much time as you need at the walk before asking for the canter. The trot isn't as helpful when teaching collection on the long-reins, so bypass it for now.

EXERCISE

1. After your horse has grasped the concept of collecting for several strides at the walk, let him relax and walk on out into a larger circle. He has felt bunched up and restrained, so let him shake loose his muscles and trot, then canter.

TROUBLESHOOTING

Speed Control within the Gait

- If your horse is having trouble, try bringing him onto a smaller circle around you. Levels One and Two were all about building communication, and you should be able to trust him quite close to you by this point. Once he is there, ask for him to shorten stride again. Often, just being closer to his handler automatically makes a horse feel less like running free, and the tighter turn of a smaller circle will naturally make him want to minimize his length of stride, as well.

- If your horse slows rather than shortens stride and breaks gait, use a tap of your whip to hustle his feet faster. When he has regained forward momentum, try asking for him to collect again. It may take several tries, but he will eventually understand what you are asking him to do.

- Sometimes, when you start working on speed control in the circle, a horse will get sloppy going around and seem to forget the basics. It seems like to fit the new lesson in, some of the earlier ones get forgotten. Don't worry, this is temporary. A horse can only focus on one thing at a time, and sometimes when he's trying hard to learn something new, easy tasks slip. In these cases, a quick refresher usually fixes things. For instance, it is common for a horse to start dropping his inside shoulder into the circle, rather than curving his body properly around the arc (fig. 8.2). In this case, step back from the Speed Control exercise for a bit. Use your inside rein to reinforce precision at a walk to remind your horse how to travel correctly on a circle. Then, send him around the circle at faster speeds with accuracy in mind, not collection. When you revisit Speed Control afterward, you will usually find he minds his shoulders much better and is smoother around the circle.

8.2   *One common problem that can crop up when working on the Speed Control exercise is for the horse to drop his inside shoulder, rather than maintaining the correct bending shape from nose to tail around the circle. When this happens, go back to a walk and use your inside rein to reestablish the circle he should know very well by now.*

- Another problem horses can develop in these exercises is rooting the nose out and down in an attempt to evade pressure and take the reins away from you. The fix is to practice lots of simple transitions. Walk to halt, walk to trot. And then do it again. It all reminds him that he needs to give to rein pressure and not get bothered and run through it. Usually, this reminder will correct the issue without much fuss.

2. While he is cantering calmly and freely around you is a good time to sort out your reins. Remember from back in Level One, it is important to recognize and take advantage of moments during training that let you untangle your reins from between your feet before they become a knotted mess. You could stop at any time to take care of this, but it's good habit to learn to sort them on the go. The way you prefer to manage your equipment during training sessions isn't as important as staying safe and setting yourself up for success. In Level Three, many exercises will have multiple parts, so it's more important to sort out reins *during* the exercises, instead of just between them.

3. When you are ready to try collection at the canter, begin by stepping in toward your horse, simultaneously shortening up on the reins (fig. 8.3). He should shorten his canter stride in response. If he slows too much, and drops to a trot, don't make a big deal of it or panic. Just bring his speed back up into the canter and try again. The issue will resolve itself once your horse understands the lesson.

4. When you ask for collection again, you may need to hold your long-reins in one hand and whip in the other. This will make it easier for you to signal with the rein hand to collect, while encouraging him forward with the whip. If his feet are still sticking or slowing too much, try using slightly less rein and more whip when you cue.

5. Once your horse has the concept of collecting for a few strides, gradually increase the number of strides you ask him to shorten, until he can do a full circle. Then, you can further advance the exercise by spiraling him in and out while collected. Don't forget to go in both directions!

Controlled Transitions

Once you have a measure of speed control within the gait with your horse, it's time to work on transitions between the gaits. You have been working on "gathering the horse up," which shortens his stride and slows him down, although with forward energy always apparent. Now, you need to balance that "contained energy" by letting him shake any tension out. So, this is a great time to perfect snappy upward transitions because the horse is probably inclined to move out at this point anyway.

A common mistake people often make when asking for speed is to let the horse decide when to drop back down to a different gait. You also don't want to have to chase your horse around to force him into a higher gear. Instead, you'd like to ask for speed and have the horse immediately step off with a willing attitude. The solution all boils down to respect. This is what gives you cleaner, faster responses. You should be able to hurry your horse off or slow him with a very small cue.

By finding an advantageous time to ask for speed—like after collection work, when a horse is primed to spring forward—you are setting yourself up for a fluid, willing transition. Then, you can later asking for upward transitions when the horse isn't so full of forward energy and still get a snappy response.

8.3 *Dan steps toward Swampy, at the same time shortening his long-reins to ask for three collected canter strides before allowing the horse to once again move out at a relaxed, neutral pace.*

EXERCISE

1. We like to have horses in a medium-sized circle for upward transitions. Too small, and it's too hard for a horse to maintain speed. Too large, and you can't use your lunge whip to tap him forward if he balks at moving right off. Being too far away is often why we end up chasing our horses into a sluggish upward transition. If we aren't close enough to reinforce a tiny cue with stronger signals, he knows he can get away with ignoring us. Bring him in closer to teach, then send him back out to test his responsiveness.

2. As you finish Speed Control at the walk, ask him to move into the trot or canter immediately from three collected strides (fig. 8.4.)

8.4 *After a lot of practice collecting within one gait, it is mentally and physically refreshing to let the horse back out on a larger circle to practice transitions be-tween gaits. Here, Swampy moves forward promptly on cue into a balanced trot following Speed Control at the walk.*

3. The second part of respect in Controlled Transitions is to anticipate and ask for a slower gait before he downshifts into it by himself. This way, you make the transition *your* idea, not his, reinforcing you as leader. So after a few strides in the higher gear, ask your horse to return to walk before setting up the exercise for another transition. One tip, don't speed up for

too long. Right now, the point is to practice transitions, not going around in one gait or another. So, move between gaits often and they will get smoother with practice.

Adding Obstacles

By this time, you have worked on a number of strengthening exercises to build toward collection in Level Three. You have asked your horse to tighten his muscles so he can be ready to change direction or speed in a moment's notice. In the next chapter, we will advance that concept with lateral work. However, before we get to that, we'd like to introduce some obstacle training.

Previously, we implemented a form of obstacle exercises when we introduced cones in several exercises (see pp. 66 and 97). We used them to weave the horse around, as well as to mark circular patterns. Now, you will introduce ground poles, which will teach the horse to step over an obstacle (fig. 8.5). Why? The answer is twofold: First, it allows your horse to relax, mentally and physically, because he has a chance to extend and you will be providing minimal cues as he, as independently as possible, thinks his way through these exercises. Second, to go any further with collection, your horse needs to be very aware of how he uses his feet. For those that don't naturally have that talent, obstacles can be an engaging, low key way to teach it.

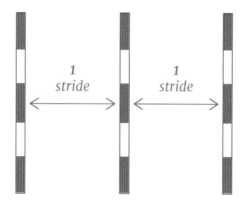

8.5 *Adding ground poles to your lesson allows your horse to relax after intensive work on collecting and helps him become more aware of how he uses his feet. After introducing the idea with a single ground pole, align a few in a row with one stride distance between each.*

EXERCISE

1. Begin with a single ground pole.

2. Either driving from behind or circling from the *center position*, ask your horse to walk over it. If all you hear is a cadenced footfall, great. But, if you hear clicking as his hooves brush over the pole, your horse is shuffling or tripping over his feet. Fortunately, both issues are an easy fix, and remedied with the same cure: keep at it. With practice, your horse will be able to coordinate his steps and learn to lift his feet higher to avoid contact. Nobody likes stubbing a toe, even when it doesn't hurt, so this should be a fast lesson.

3. When your horse has figured out a single pole, lay a few of them in a line, parallel to each other. Space them a stride apart, which you can measure by your horse's hoofprints in the dirt.

4. Track directly behind him as he navigates the poles, guiding him as little as possible. Once he can step through at a walk and trot without ticking one, it's time to up this challenge.

Advancing the Exercise:

Adding Obstacles—Distance and Height

You have a couple of options for advancing this exercise, and while you should do both, it doesn't matter the order you choose.

1. Add more ground poles, and arrange them in varied shapes and distances. For example, arc them on a circle of travel, so the ends closer to where you stand in the center are closer together and the ends on the outside of the circle are farther apart. Or, vary the spacing between a series of poles so your horse has to lengthen and shorten his stride accordingly to get through them. You can get quite creative with this step. Maybe you zigzag the poles, and long-rein your horse from directly behind in a serpentine shape over them (figs. 8.6 A–C).

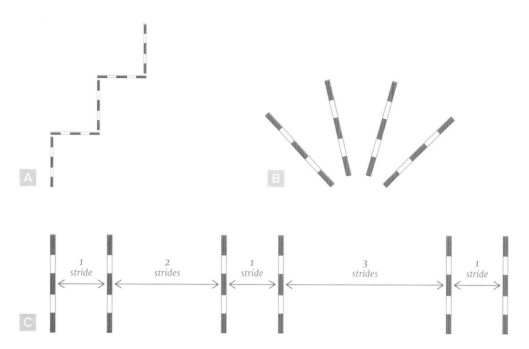

8.6 A–C   *Once your horse is working over a few poles with even distances between them, you can increase the challenge by adding poles and arranging them in different shapes (A), with varying distances (B), or in patterns that test both your skills, like a zigzag you need to serpentine over (C).*

2. Once your horse is competent working over poles on the ground, it is time to add another challenge: elevation. To do this, go back to a simple setup of a few poles, and use low blocks under each end to raise them a few inches off the ground. This will really help your horse concentrate on his footwork, to keep from banging his legs on a pole.

3. The final advancement of obstacle work is small jumps, created by raising your poles just a bit more. You aren't looking for too much height, just enough so that he isn't able to just step over them. You want him to have to put a bit of effort into it, and actually jump each one.

4. If you are having fun with this, or just want to take the *Obstacle Training* exercise outside on a nice day, you can use found objects instead of poles. Fallen logs can work well (fig. 8.7). This is another area where you can get creative, but be sure to use common sense: stay safe when assembling obstacles and don't overchallenge your horse.

8.7 *You can take Obstacle Training outside the arena and use natural obstacles to further challenge you and your horse—as well as have a little fun.*

What's Next?

Once your horse has mastered *Speed Control within the Gaits* and *Transitions* between them, and is stepping lightly over different arrangements of ground poles, you are ready to progress to more serious lateral work. That is where we are headed next.

9
Advanced Lateral Work

Welcome to Advanced Lateral Work. This collection of exercises is the most advanced in the Double Dan long-reining levels. By the time you finish this chapter, you will have good control moving your horse's shoulders and hips, lessons that will translate directly to under-saddle work. The lateral work builds to advanced maneuvers, like flying lead changes, which we cover later.

For this chapter and onward, you can set aside your lunge whip. Everything from here on out will be done in close quarters with the horse—by now you should feel comfortable breaching the Red Zone—and a carriage whip is more appropriate (fig. 9.1). All other tack is the same as before: bridle with bit, Lungie Bungie, two long-reins attached directly to the bit, and a roller.

9.1 *For the duration of this and the final exercises in this book, you and your horse will be working in close quarters.*

Lateral Movements on the Fence

For this exercise, as with earlier beginning lateral work, you need a long, straight fence. An arena or sturdy pasture fence will do. Like earlier exercises, the fence will serve as a visual guide and physical barrier for your horse as you reintroduce lateral movements (fig. 9.2).

If you recall, we first discussed using fences for lateral motion at the end of Level One when you worked on Lateral Yield (p. 73) and again with Intermediate Lateral Movement (p. 103). To review Lateral Yield: you follow the horse at a walk down the fence line. Then, you loosen the rein *away* from the fence

9.2 *You will need a long straight barrier as an aid to begin Lateral Movements on the Fence. It doesn't need to be fancy. Any pasture or arena fence will do, as long as it's straight, sturdy, and can serve as a visual guide.*

as you simultaneously gather the rein *nearest* the fence. The pressure tips the horse's nose into the fence and the forward momentum "drifts" his hips away from it into a three-track movement. At first, you started with only a step or two of Lateral Yield before allowing him to relax back to following the fence, then you gradually asked for more steps by tapping his hip with the whip from the ¾ position.

EXERCISE

1. To begin *Lateral Movements on the Fence*, simply ask the horse to walk parallel to the fence in both directions. You don't want him to think that every time you approach a fence, you will be asking him to move his hips or nose into or away from it. You want him to realize that it can be a relaxing, no-pressure place to be, as well as a place to work. Anytime you feel your horse getting overly tense during the following exercises, don't be afraid to allow him a breather and just follow the fence around. It will let his mind relax while keeping his body in position to pick lateral movement right back up.

2. Ask for the same three-track exercise you first learned in Level One—begin with the horse's nose to the fence while you use a whip cue to ask his hips to the inside. Your position should be similar to what you did in Level One, close to the fence while you pushed his hips away, putting you in the ¾ position. The difference between Level One and Level Three is simply the difficulty and how closely you are working to your horse. You will be much pickier about how sharply your horse steps and listens. And, because you are in tight proximity, you can make corrections much faster. You should find your horse is much better at this exercise than in Level One. His responses and reflexes should be improved. We like to start lateral work again with this Level One exercise to not only test this, but to refresh him on the concept with something familiar.

TROUBLESHOOTING

Lateral Movements on the Fence

When teaching a lesson down the fence, it is easier if you teach the horse going one way until he has learned it well in that direction, before starting the lesson over and going in the other direction. As you go around the arena or pasture, eventually, you will reach a corner, which you should simply drive your horse through. Once he has picked up momentum on the new side, you can ask for lateral movements again.

However, if you need to use the same stretch of fence for whatever reason, it will require doubling back at the corners to go the other direction. In that case, simply turn your horse in a teardrop shape off from the corner and toward the center of the arena, finally guiding him back to the fence headed the other way (fig. 9.3).

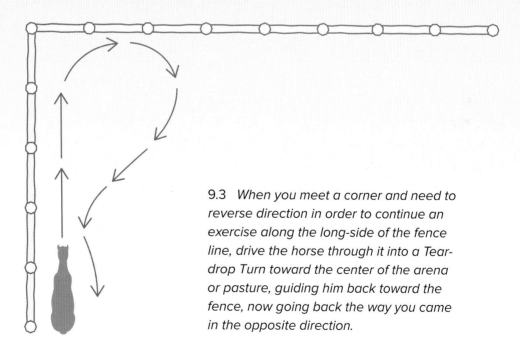

9.3 *When you meet a corner and need to reverse direction in order to continue an exercise along the long-side of the fence line, drive the horse through it into a Teardrop Turn toward the center of the arena or pasture, guiding him back toward the fence, now going back the way you came in the opposite direction.*

Leg–Yield Back to the Fence

The next thing you will work on is *Leg-Yield Back to the Fence*. In this exercise, you still ask for a three-track movement. The difference is, you are asking him to travel somewhere, from point A to B—asking him to keep his body relatively straight while he steps sideways toward and away from the fence. Your position during this exercise is directly behind him.

EXERCISE

1. Begin by following the fence as before, but a few feet farther away from it than normal.

2. Then, ask the horse to step toward the fence. Use the rein closest to the fence to tip his nose toward it, while offering a light secondary contact with your other rein to collect your horse as you practiced in the last chapter (fig. 9.4). At the same time, tap your whip to move his hips toward the inside of the arena. The whip also does double duty by encouraging forward and sideways motion. Too much rein with too little whip, and your horse's feet will lose their cadence and stop. If you get stuck or your horse misbehaves, just drive him straight back to the fence and start over.

9.4 *Begin the Leg-Yield Back to the Fence exercise a few feet off the fence-line. Tip the horse's nose to the fence while keeping a light contact with the long-rein furthest from the fence. Use your whip to move his hips to the inside of the arena or pasture while encouraging forward momentum and sideways motion.*

3. Ask your horse to yield away from the fence (figs. 9.5 A–C).

4. After four to six steps, tip the horse's nose to the inside of the arena and tap him on the inside hip to move him back toward the fence.

5. Continue down the fence, weaving both to and away from it. Your horse's hoofprints will leave a zigzag pattern in the dirt behind him as he makes his way forward.

6. When your horse is Leg-Yielding Back to the Fence smoothly at the walk, try it at the trot. Often, you will find the horse does the exercise better at a trot, because the increased forward motion helps to propel him through the maneuver. It's good to establish speed quickly, before you use up all of the length of your fence: We like to pick an end, and circle the horse; then, when he is maintaining the trot, we draw him onto a teardrop turn and into the three-track movement on the fence.

9.5 A–C *Ask your horse to yield away from the fence, maintaining his three-track position (A). Weave back to and away from the fence the length of the arena or pasture (B & C).*

When your horse has conquered Leg-Yielding Back to the Fence at a trot, you are ready for the next exercise. We should mention that all of our close-up work, with few exceptions, is done at the walk and trot. Cantering in such tight quarters is not only more dangerous, it is also physically very hard for a horse to do without quite a lot of preparation.

TROUBLESHOOTING

Leg–Yielding Back to the Fence

- Sometimes, a horse just doesn't grasp the idea of the Leg-Yield Back to the Fence. In this case, you can try an alternate way of setting him up for it that can help clarify things. An alternate way to teach Leg-Yield Back to the Fence is to show him the Teardrop Turn, which you used previously in corners to set your horse up to work the same stretch of fence in the opposite direction (see p. 139). In this exercise, you can turn him at any point, not just the corner. Start by walking a few steps following the fence at the normal distance. Then, turn your horse away from the fence into a teardrop turn. As he straightens back out facing the other direction, he is in the proper position to ask for a three-track yield back to the fence.

- When your horse yields to the fence, he might drop (or lean) his shoulder into the turn. This might not be a safety issue now, but it is sloppy foot-work. You want to correct the habit because it could be dangerous under saddle when "diving in" with a shoulder could lead to the horse losing his balance and falling, particularly at faster speeds. Reinforce good posture in the yield with increased pressure from your supporting long-rein. At the same time, bump his ribs with the carriage whip near the shoulder that is dropping. Both of these should encourage him to pick his shoulder back up and stand up straight.

Shoulder-In

Once your horse is good at three-track-ing with his nose toward the fence, it is time to reverse things with our *Shoul-der-In* exercise. We started to learn this exercise with Tail to the Fence in Level Two (p. 106).

EXERCISE

1. Begin with a nice, relaxed walk along the fence.

2. To initiate the Shoulder-In move-ment, pick up on the inside long-rein (toward the inside of the arena or pasture—so if the fence is on your right, it is your left rein), guiding the horse's nose to the middle of the arena. Tap the inside hindquarter with your carriage whip to keep forward momentum and hold his hip on the rail. This adjustment should produce the three-tracks you are looking for (fig. 9.6). As with other exercises, start with a few steps, then release him back to following the fence. Gradually, you can work up to longer distances.

9.6 *Dan and Swampy demonstrate Shoulder-In. Your horse's shoulders come to the inside (toward the center of the arena or pasture) with a signal from your inside long-rein, and his haunches remain on the path along the fence.*

Advancing the Exercise:

Shoulder-In at the Trot

After your horse can do the Shoulder-In exercise at the walk, try it at the trot. The setup is much the same as trotting Leg-Yield Back to the Fence.

EXERCISE

1. Start at one end of your fence with a trot circle to build speed.

2. Then, use a Teardrop Turn to bring your horse out of the circle and alongside the fence.

3. Once his body is traveling straight, you can ask for your horse's shoulders to come in toward the center of the arena or pasture with a touch of your inside long-rein while his hind end stays on the original path with direction from your whip and outside long-rein. As before, tempo is important, so lighten rein pressure as needed to maintain forward motion. If your horse stalls out, you could always ask for the lateral movement again, but it's harder to reinvigorate sticky feet.

Advanced Lateral Movement

In our final exercise for this series, *Advanced Lateral Movement,* you ask the horse to do something that is quite challenging: bend his nose and hip in the same direction. This exercise sets him up quite well for high-level, under-saddle maneuvers that are used in both English and Western disciplines.

Up to this point, when you have independently moved the nose and hip, it's been in the opposite direction, as when yielding down the fence. This is quite easy for the horse, since his body most naturally moves that way. Now, in a two-part lesson, you are going to ask for his nose and hip to move closer together on one side while he is in motion. The only other time thus far you have requested this is in your work in the circle when centrifugal forces help him stay in the correct shape, bending from nose to tail.

However, in Advanced Lateral Movement, you do not have the help of a circle. All the workload in holding form is on the horse's muscles. Every exercise up to this point should have helped ensure your horse is fit enough and trained enough to perform this type of collection. So let's begin.

EXERCISE

1. Start by walking your horse down the fence, with you in the ¾ position on his inside (toward the center of the arena or pasture) hip. Unless you need to increase forward motion by driving from behind during the exercise, this is the position where you will stay throughout.

2. Initiate the lateral movement by tipping the horse's nose slightly into the arena using your inside rein. As before, to prevent him from mistaking this signal to mean he should turn into a circle, use your outside rein as light support to keep him moving down the fence.

3. At the same time as your rein cue, tap his ribs nearest you, which will prompt him to bend them away from you, toward the fence. When he does this, you will notice it also has the effect of tipping his hips slightly to the inside of the arena. As with earlier lessons, only ask for a step or two before letting him relax and extend, following the rail at a walk.

4. This is a very difficult exercise for most horses to achieve, but it is doable. It actually is one of the few where sitting astride is an advantage, as your legs work well to help hold the horse in place. In long-reining, you are relying on only your rein- and whip-handling skills, as well as body position, to encourage your horse along. However, if you can accomplish the maneuver here, it should be relatively simple to replicate under saddle.

5. The next phase of the Advanced Lateral Movement exercise takes the challenge up a notch: Instead of starting off walking down the fence, set your horse up with a Teardrop Turn at the end of the arena (see p. 139).

6. As soon as your horse straightens from the curve of the turn and is headed toward the fence, ask for his head and hip to bend to the inside of the arena with the inside rein, and tap his ribs on the inside, too. This will step him to the rail forward and sideways, with his body bent away from the

direction of travel. This is much like a three-track, only we aren't as picky about his footfalls as we are that he travels with his body shaped correctly. It takes a lot of trust for a horse to blindly step in a direction you ask, which is what you are asking of him here (fig. 9.7). This is where your preparation from the previous two levels really reveals how well you have learned communication and feel.

9.7 *Advanced Lateral Movement is difficult for the horse—he must give you both his nose and his hip, and step forward and sideways almost blindly in the direction you are telling him to travel with your outside long-rein cues and whip-handling.*

Remember to be patient and don't overuse your whip in an effort to get too many steps at a time. Build up slowly and you will actually find your training goes faster than if you try to rush things. And you will have a much happier student!

TROUBLESHOOTING

Advanced Lateral Movement

Often, when you first ask the horse to tip both his nose and hip to the inside of the arena, there are a few common problems that can arise. Here's how to negotiate them.

- The first issue seen is a failure of the horse to yield either his nose or his hip. They both stem from a lack of respect or worry about the new maneuver and so should be handled much the same. With them, you will notice resistance to a cue, then the exercise will fall apart because he will either get tense and upset or just ignore you. For a horse that evades or "tunes out" the inside rein (toward the center of the arena or pasture), lift your hand higher when cueing; then, drive him forward with a stronger whip cue. This should loosen up head and neck tension. If not, go back and work on earlier exercises until he is soft and willingly giving his nose again. When it is the hip that won't yield, switch to a stronger signal. Instead of tapping the inside ribs, try the outside hip. Sometimes horses just need a more direct cue about the body part they should be moving, and where. If your horse still ignores you, increase the pressure gradually until you get one good step. Then, try again, with a lighter hip cue.

- The other issue seen when first starting the Advanced Lateral Movement exercise is the horse wandering off the fence. In this case, drive him back up to the fence and don't make a big deal out of it. If he is trying and making an effort to do what you ask, don't pick at him. Sometimes, a horse is thinking so hard about placing his nose and hips, he forgets about his feet. As your horse gets more comfortable responding to the new combination of cues and holding this pose, his path will get straighter all on its own. He just needs time and practice.

Continued ▶

- Your horse might drop his shoulder. It is a very natural mistake. He is already leading his body with the shoulder and it is a very small leap to lean his weight into the same direction. You will encounter a similar setup when you ask for flying lead changes (see p. 154), so you don't want to establish bad habits so late in the game here, when you've been so careful to avoid them so far. Fortunately, the solution is not difficult. Release the horse's nose and drive his inside hip forward up underneath him. When his weight is balanced in his hindquarters instead of falling heavily on the front end, you can ask for the nose and hip to take their places again. Repeat this fix as needed until he is consistently moving off in good form.

Now that you have the lateral work series well in hand, you have all the tools in place to tackle our final two long-reining exercises. Discover these in the next chapter.

10

Pinwheels and Flying Lead Changes

Welcome to our final long-reining lessons! At this point, you have developed a strong communication with your horse and he should have reached quite a high fitness level. The following two exercises, *Pinwheels* and *Flying Lead Changes*, will give you maximum control over your horse's movement, down to each individual footfall. Master them, and you will be ready to take on the highest levels of under-saddle work or long-reining.

You are now ready to attempt some pretty advanced maneuvers off the fence, in the middle of your arena or pasture. However, if at any point you find a weakness in your horse's execution of the exercises, don't be afraid to return to the fence to sharpen his skills. When you return to the new exercises with the basics well in hand, he will do them with more confidence and cadence.

You will still be using your carriage whip and positioned closely to your horse throughout. If you had attempted these lessons earlier in our long-reining program, it would have been unsafe, but by now, you and your horse have built a level of trust and communication that makes work in close quarters possible. If at any time you feel insecure about this, don't be afraid to revisit earlier lessons to reestablish respect.

Pinwheel

Like many of the other exercises you've now learned that focus on collection, the *Pinwheel* exercise sharpens your horse's shoulder control. In fact, when we have a horse that consistently drops his shoulder during our lateral work series (see p. 148), we'll sometimes stop and introduce this exercise right then. It is first taught at the walk, then at the trot.

EXERCISE

1. Begin the exercise with a basic walk circle around you.

2. Once the horse has free, forward movement, switch from using your whip on his *inside* hip (inside the circle), which indicates forward movement, to tapping it on the *outside* hip to encourage his hindquarter to step off the path toward you (fig. 10.1). Prevent a turn or forward movement off the circle by supporting his nose with your inside rein. This is a high level of rein and whip management, and it may take some time on your part to get the coordination down. Be patient!

3. The ultimate goal is to have the horse maintain the same circle, but instead of following his nose around it, he faces away as well as stepping sideways and forward, somewhere between a three-track movement and a side-pass. You stand in the same spot throughout: first in the center

10.1   *From the basic circle, ask your horse to bring his hind end in toward you with a whip cue on his outside hip. Dan is supporting Swampy with his inside long-rein as the horse swings into position at the walk. The ultimate goal is to have Swampy continue the same circle, but instead of following his nose around it, to face away and step sideways and forward, somewhere between a three- track movement and a side-pass. At first, ask for small movements of the hip to the inside, then let him relax back onto the basic circle.*

position as he picks up the circle, then directly behind as he transitions into pinwheeling around you.

4. Be sure to practice circling both ways, and in this exercise switching directions should be fluid, without any starts or stops: Ask for the change of direction after you release your horse from a *Pinwheel* back to the basic circle. As soon as his body straightens and forward motion picks up, pick up on your outside rein to redirect him into an outside turn and back onto the circle facing the other way. You will probably need to use the whip to encourage forward motion throughout the turn, but exactly where will depend on your horse. By now, you should be reading him well enough to know which of his feet are getting sticky and can cue that one to keep the energy up.

Advancing the Exercise:

Pinwheel at the Trot

Once you and your horse have the concept at the walk, we like to quickly move up to doing the *Pinwheel* exercise at the trot. A horse will often find doing this lesson easier at the faster gait because the extra momentum helps carry him through each motion.

EXERCISE

1. Begin by establishing a trot circle. You will probably need to send the horse a bit farther from you to allow him the freedom to pick up some speed.

2. Then, start gathering your reins *Hand Over Fist* and slowly decrease the size of his circle until you can easily cue him with your carriage whip. If he is still stepping around with good momentum, begin feeling his mouth with your inside rein by shortening it. He should yield his nose willingly and tip it toward you slightly. You don't need much bend: the point is to prevent excessive forward motion when you ask him to transition into the pinwheel.

3. Initiate the pinwheel by tapping your horse's outside hip to drive his hind legs underneath him and sideways into the circle. Because of centrifugal force, he should find the motion much easier to accomplish at the trot than the walk (fig. 10.2 A & B).

10.2 A & B *When your horse is competent doing the Pinwheel at the walk, quickly progress to the trot as horses often find this lesson easier at the faster gait, because the extra momentum helps carry him through each motion. Allow him to gain speed on a larger circle before reeling him in Hand Over Fist, shortening the inside rein, and tapping the outside hip with the whip to cue the hindquarter to step over and in (A). Ask for more sideways steps with a greater degree of angle to the hips. Eventually, you will have him rotating freely around you, with his shoulders moving slightly faster than his hind end to maintain the circle shape. You remain in position, so as your horse moves, your center position becomes directly behind, as Dan shows here with Swampy (B).*

TROUBLESHOOTING

Pinwheel

- Your horse will not have a straight body when he learns the Pinwheel exercise. And, as with previous lessons, don't expect too many steps from him at first—just ask for small movements of the hip to the inside, then release him back to going forward around the circle. Later, ask for more sideways steps with a greater degree of angle to the hips. Eventually, you will have him rotating freely around you, with his shoulders moving slightly faster than his hind end to maintain the circle shape.

- It is important to not lose all forward motion during the Pinwheel, which can cause all of your momentum to disappear. You've worked hard to "bring the life up" in his feet and don't want to have to reestablish it if you don't have to. It's a lot easier to maintain it, instead. That's where forward movement can help. If your horse were very advanced at this exercise, you might ask him to only step sideways around the circle, but you are not looking for that level of refinement here. Right now, you want to help your horse succeed by keeping a bit of forward movement. This will require you to move your feet and follow him as he circles around you. If forward motion is ever lost, chances are all motion is gone too, at this stage. The

Flying Lead Changes

In our final exercise, we will be introducing Flying Lead Changes. Everything you have worked on so far comes into play in this one exercise, from quality canter circles to lateral movements down the fence and to the Pinwheel exercise you just learned. You might find that when the horse can consistently do flying lead changes in the long-reins, teaching him to do them trick is to catch it happening soon enough that you can fix it before his feet stop moving completely. If they do, you have to start all over with the exercise, establishing a circle then asking for the maneuver. But, if you can correct him as soon as you notice him losing steam—using your whip and reins to bring him back to a basic circle—you can reset a new Pinwheel easily.

- If your horse still has trouble performing the pinwheel, go back to the Lateral Work on the Fence to clarify the movements you are asking for. Having a physical barrier often helps guide the horse sideways, but when you take that barrier away, it can leave some horses feeling lost. Plus, when you add in extra rein cues to keep forward motion in check, and you can quickly escalate a horse's frustration in a Pinwheel. So, don't hesitate to review. Get the fence work very solid. Then come right back to Pinwheels. Often, once you get the horse thinking strongly about stepping his feet sideways instead of forward down the fence, he will automatically pick up the same motion when you take him immediately off it and ask with the same cues. That is where a quality Pinwheel begins, without a big fight or tugging on his face to maintain frame. Remember, one good step is all you need from him before you release the pressure and praise him.

under saddle will be a snap, because you will have leg cues to reinforce what you are asking.

By now, your horse should have the physical strength needed to perform small cantering circles, and the training to keep you both safe. You use the same tack as the last exercise, and still signal with a carriage whip. It is important to note that this exercise can be very tiring on even fit horses, so take your time. Don't expect perfection the first day. It may take a while for your horse to be able to do each step, and that's just fine.

EXERCISE

1. Start with a circle. It may be easier to send him away from you on a largish circle to establish the canter, then draw him in, or you can initiate a closer circle at a trot and bump him up into a canter there. Do whatever works best with your individual horse. The end goal is the same: we want him holding the canter with good forward motion on a small circle around us (fig. 10.3). Chances are, your horse will take some practice to do this first step. By this time, he knows what to do, and it will just take time to grow his endurance and strength to meet the challenge. You can help him with light support from your inside rein and driving him on by tapping the whip at his inside hind leg.

2. The Pinwheel exercise should have prepared you well for what's next. It forced you to quickly change whip and rein to cue the horse's hip to the inside. Although many people think Flying Lead Changes are a shoulder movement because they can see the front legs change, it is actually initiated in the horse's hips, as well. For the purposes of our example, let's say your horse is going to the left and is on the left lead. You want to switch to the right, and the easiest way to teach this is to have your horse associate it with a direction change. You have worked hard up to this point to prevent him dropping his inside

10.3 *Your horse should have the strength to perform small cantering circles. This is integral to Flying Lead Changes. This size circle can be tiring for any horse, so take your time teaching this first step. Support the horse on the circle with inside rein and your whip at his inside hip, as Dan is doing here.*

shoulder, and this exercise is one reason why. He must stay very straight in the shoulders to perform a flying lead change cleanly and precisely. To initiate the change, direct him to turn his inside hip into the circle, just like the Pinwheel (fig. 10.4).

3.   However, instead of limiting forward motion, let him now leave the path of the circle. Be prepared to follow, and as soon as his body is in a straight line, direct him right onto a new circle. He should switch leads then to the right, as well.

10.4 *To initiate a Flying Lead Change, direct your horse's hip into the circle, as Dan is doing with Swampy here. You may note this is just like the beginning of the Pinwheel exercise. However, instead of limiting forward motion, Dan will allow Swampy to now leave the circle and redirect him onto a new circle going to the right, which should prompt a change of leads.*

Advancing the Exercise:

Flying Lead Changes on a Straight Line

Once your horse is easily changing leads as you move from a circle in one direction to a circle in another, it's time to ask him to try the changes on a straight line. Of course, your horse won't immediately be switching every stride, like a Lipizzaner or higher level dressage horse, but he can get there, with this exercise and time. For less lofty goals, learning to change leads on a straight line will help in many English and Western disciplines where flying lead changes are either required maneuvers or ensure the horse remains balanced with his feet under him.

EXERCISE

1. Start with a cantering circle again. When he has good cadence, ask again for the Pinwheel, then let him drift forward.

2. Whereas before you immediately tipped him into a circle going the other way to switch leads, now you are going to give him the chance to try it on a straight line. This is important to learn, because it teaches the horse he can change leads without necessarily going in a new direction. It also helps to keep his shoulders nicely centered, so eventually, you could change leads as often as you want without having to reset his body after it has dropped into a turn.

3. Give your horse a stride or two then ask for the change: Pick up rein contact on both sides to shift his weight back, and tap his hips the direction you want the switch to go. If he is on the right lead, tap his right hip to encourage the hindquarters to move left. This should instigate the change to the left behind, and his front feet should then change automatically.

4. As soon as the change is made, drive him forward. As with our earlier exercises, losing momentum will put an end to your hard work and you will have to reset the exercise. Once forward motion is established, you can take him into a circle to the left to reinforce the lead your horse just changed to—and it also gives you a breather after chasing him all over the arena.

TROUBLESHOOTING

Flying Lead Changes

If advanced flying lead changes sound difficult, it's because they are. Even if your horse is a bright and willing student, things can go wrong. There are many reasons a horse won't change leads.

- Some are physical, and some horses just favor one side over another. In these cases, you will need to build up their fitness on the weak side to balance the strong one, then try lead changes again.

- If it's a lack of training, go back and review the lateral work series and Pinwheels. These are paramount to your horse having the pieces to create a quality lead change.

- If your horse is solid in those exercises and his fitness is up to par, the problem isn't educational background or physical training—it's just a mental block. For whatever reason, your horse doesn't feel ready to do flying lead changes or doesn't understand what you're asking. *Counter-cantering*, or cantering a circle on the wrong lead, often helps this. Usually, when a horse canters to the left, he picks up the left lead, and the same to the right. It is simply the easiest way to travel a circle at a canter for him, and the most natural. However, he is fully capable of going around to the left on the right lead, and vice-versa. In fact, some horses that favor one side too strongly always do this going in their weak direction. But, most horses do not because it is more demanding on them to do so.

However, if you have a horse counter-canter a circle, it will make a lead change a relief. Counter-canter is very difficult to do, so is a lesson in itself. However, once your horse can do it, he will find flying lead changes easy. Indirectly, it should resolve the issue. In fact, he will likely be asking *you* to do a lead change because it is suddenly the easiest option. And, you go from being the bad guy who's annoying him with flying lead changes, to the good guy who lets him do one.

EXERCISE

1. Set up the counter-canter by asking your horse onto a canter circle, as normal. In this example, we'll say to the right.

2. Pinwheel him around and send him off the circle, just as you would for a lead change. Instead of tapping his hips left to initiate the change, think back to when you asked your horse to tip his nose and hip in the same direction down the fence in Advanced Lateral Movement (see p. 144). You will be asking for the same motion here, but without a fence to hold him, and he will naturally track onto a circle going left, which is what you want. Initiate the lateral movement by tipping the horse's nose slightly to the right using your inside rein. To prevent him mistaking this signal as one to turn right, use your outside rein as support to guide him left.

3. At the same time as your rein cue, tap his ribs on the right, which will prompt him to bend them toward the left circle while encouraging him to maintain his right lead. Ideally, he will travel a few strides that way until you release the pressure and cue him to change leads to the left. Usually, horses are more than ready to comply because counter-cantering is so taxing on them.

4. If your horse loses the counter-canter, just set it up again. Keep practicing until he can hold it for up to a full revolution around the circle. If he has built up that much strength and coordination, he is probably physically able to do most anything you need. But, counter-cantering will never be his preference over cantering on the correct lead, so it shouldn't be any problem to ask for the switch at any point.

5. Once you can get a Flying Lead Change using the counter-canter fix, try it again on the straight line. He may change directions with the lead change, and try to pick up a new circle. That's fine in the beginning—with time, you can ask him to change leads, keeping his body straighter. Eventually, he will maintain his forward path while changing leads, and at that point, you can start asking for multiple lead changes. But again, progress slowly.

Level Three Wrap-Up

In a way, Level Three is never "finished"—you can always practice these exercises (as well as the more elementary ones from Levels One and Two) to keep your horse engaged, to address any issues you might be having in the saddle on the ground first, to condition him, or simply to have a little fun. However, over time you and your horse should gradually master these more advanced lessons, and eventually you should be able to review the following smoothly and with finesse, anytime you want:

- On a circle, ask the horse to shorten and lengthen his stride at the walk and canter.

- Perform instant and controlled upward and downward transitions through all three gaits.

- Navigate over ground poles and natural obstacles.

- Leg-Yield from the fence into the middle of the arena and back again in a zigzag pattern.

- Shoulder-In at the walk and trot, and Advanced Lateral Movement on and off the fence.

- Pinwheel at both the walk and trot, with the horse maintaining a circle while facing away from you and stepping sideways.

- Flying lead changes on a straight line.

So what next? Turn the page to find out where you can go with your horse's long-reining education after Level Three.

11

Moving On

Congratulations! You have completed every bit of the Double Dan Long-Reining program.

You may recall that in the beginning, we listed several reasons an everyday horse owner should embark on this journey.

1. Bridging the gap between halter and lead to bridle and saddle.

2. Educating a young horse. You can start building muscles and learning *before* he is physically ready for the weight of a rider. You can build muscles in his back and neck in preparation for a rider as part of starting under saddle.

3. When you are an under-confident rider, but still want to start teaching your horse under-saddle maneuvers from the safety of the ground.

4. Re-educating older horses. Long-reining allows you to teach and correct them from the safety of the ground.

5. Troubleshooting problems and educating yourself to better, more seamless communication with a horse.

Did you see improvement in the areas you were aiming to work on? We hope you got that and more out of our long-reining exercises, and that they set you and your horse up for whatever is ahead. You should have noticed a greater level of communication and willingness in your horse, as well as an increase in feel and patience in yourself. Proper training takes all of these, so you are sure to have cultivated them along the way, as well as a few other benefits.

After Level Three

The big question is, where do you go from here? The answer depends on you. If you want to teach your horse tricks on the long-reins, such as bowing or lying down, this is a great time. There are many resources available to help you grow your long-reining knowledge from here.

If you are ready to take on saddle training in earnest, like most of our students who reach this point, we have a DVD series that can help you on your way. Our *Body Control Basics under Saddle* expands on our long-reining lessons to mold your horse into a soft and responsive partner when riding. The exercises in the DVDs develop control of the five main body parts: the head, neck, shoulders, rib cage, and hips.

You already have a wonderful leg up with the long-reining exercises, which will make the under-saddle work progress much faster. In the riding series, your horse will progress to carrying you through beautiful circles, smooth canter departures, flawless lead changes. You can find these, as well as our other instructional DVDs and our long-reining equipment at our website, doubledan-horsemanship.com. There, you will also find a calendar of upcoming clinics and shows we will be at throughout Australia and North America. We look forward to seeing you down the road!

Acknowledgments

Thank you to the trainers who have helped us
in the art of long-reining:

Dan James' dad, George James
Heath Harris
Clay Maier
Carole Mercer
Bo Jena

Index

Page numbers in *italics* indicate illustrations.